ANTHOLOGY
—of—
ONE

1990-2007
Collected Poems of J.L. Hittle

Also by J.L. Hittle...

Nexus

The Rhythm of Life

An Everlasting Mark

Coffee Shop Cadence

I Strain

A Carousel of Days

ANTHOLOGY
—of—
ONE

1990-2007
Collected Poems of J.L. Hittle

BROKEN ARROW PUBLISHING, LLC

ANTHOLOGY
—of—
ONE

1990-2007
Collected Poems of J.L. Hittle

All rights reserved.
Copyright © 2008 by J.L. Hittle

All rights reserved.
Printed in the United States of America.
No part of this book may be reproduced in any form or by any electronic or mechanical means, including information storage and retrieval systems, without permission in writing from the copyright owner.

For information or to correspond with the author, please address:

BROKEN ARROW PUBLISHING, LLC

157 Woodman Avenue
Saco, Maine 04072

ISBN 978-0-9709976-3-0

For Julia

Contents...

THE BEGINNING	1
I ALONE	2
A WORD WITHHELD	3
A FATHER IS TOLD THAT HIS SON IS DEAD, AND THEN TOLD HE IS THE WRONG FATHER	4
A GUY SAYS TO ME	5
A RENTAL TRUCK FILLED WITH FERTILIZER	6
A THREE-LEGGED DOG NAMED HOOVER	7
A YOUNG PRESIDENT	8
I HAD OTHER PLANS FOR MY LIFE	9
THE SPACES BETWEEN	10
LITTLE PINK COAT	11
BONE UPON BONE	12
CALLING TO ARTHUR	13
CARNIVAL SEVENTEEN	14
CARPE DIEM	15
CORN	16
"YOU LOOK JUST LIKE YOUR FATHER"	17
DEATH BY A THOUSAND CUTS	18
DESCRIBING A RAINBOW TO A BLIND MAN	19
DIFFERENCE QUANTIFIED	20
DIVINITY	21
CONSIDERING HE WAS SUPPOSED TO BE IN PRISON	22
ECHOES OF EMILY	23
EXPLOITED TO FEEL LOVED	24
HALF?	25
FOOLS' FRIENDS	26
GIFTS YOU CAN'T BUY	27
MY PARTICLES WILL COALESCE	28
HAPPY BIRTHDAY, ROOM 202	29
I DIE	30
I DOUBT	31
I ENVY	32
I FORGET	33
I GRIEVE	34

I HAVE LEARNED	35
I HOPE	36
THE HUNGER OF HOPE	37
I LEARN	38
I LIKE THIS POEM	39
HE DREAMED OF RISING IN A NEW YORK FLAT	40
I MIGHT	41
IF I WERE BLACK	42
I THIRST	43
WORDS LABEL UNTIL THEY OFFEND	44
I, PRONOUN	45
HOW SWEET THE CRUST	46
INNOCENCE LOST	47
THE HUNGRY WAVES	48
A DAY'S WORTH OF SNIPPETS	50
SQUIRREL INDECISION	53
I IMAGINE	54
IN VINO VERITAS	55
IN LINE AT THE GROCERY STORE	56
JOB SECURITY	57
JANUARY 1, 2001	58
MAGNUM OPUS	59
MAGGOTS	60
NONE OF THIS IS TRUE	61
MY HEART, MY HEAT, MY WONDER	62
NERO'S ANACOLUTHON	63
PARADISE	64
OUT OF LIFE ITSELF	65
PUT A CORK IN IT	66
RELICS	67
WE ALL FALL DEAD	68
PLOUGHSHARES	69
PHYSICAL	70
SIMILE	71
THE CENTURIES CLOSE, ONE AFTER ANOTHER	72
THE ADULTERER WAKES	73
THE ANSWER TO YOUR QUESTION	74

THE HEART OF THE MATTER	75
THE MACHINE	76
THE POET'S INK	77
THE MEN IN THE MIRROR	78
THE ONE THAT GOT AWAY	79
THE THRUSHES' THREE	80
HARVEST OF SHAME	81
TREASURES WITHOUT KEYS	82
THE REST	83
THRENODY ON LOSS	84
STEPPING IN YOUR OWN GUM	85
TRACKS	86
VILLANELLE FOR LAURIE (MY SISTER FOUND A GRAY)	87
AND TALK ABOUT THE WEATHER	88
WALKING ON WATER	89
WHEN THE PAST KILLS THE FUTURE	90
YON YEN	91
SMUGGLERS' DENIAL	92
TEENAGE LOVE	93
BREATHLESS IN MAINE	94
MARCIA'S FACE WAS OILY	95
A FARMER SURVIVED	96
MY CAPISTRANO	97
HOLY MACKEREL	98
ESPECIALLY BOURBON	99
I FLY	100
NURSE!	102
THE GORILLAS' SIDE	104
THE MAGIC CONFLUENCE	106
THE MAGIC KITE	108
THE LAST TIME MY FATHER LEFT	110
I STRAIN	111
DREADED WASH DAY	112
MY SWEET STILL LOVES ME	113
A CONVERSATION WITH MY FATHER	114
FISHING WITH DAD	115
SLEEPWALKING AT CHRISTMASTIME	116

FIRST AND LAST	117
WAKE ME FOR DINNER	118
MEMORIES OF THE GAME	119
LONGING FOR RECESS	121
METAPHORICALLY SPEAKING: A BASEBALL PLAYER MEETS A GIRL AT CLOSING TIME	122
FAMILY KISSES	123
BRUSH STROKES	126
THE OPRAH WINFREY SONG	127
WHEN I FOUND THE PLAYBOY	129
UPON READING AN AD FOR PENIS NLARGEMENT	130
VEGETABLE LOGIC	131
A RECIPE FOR RESTAURANTS	132
JUST DO IT	133
I LIVE TO SLEEP	134
HOITY-TOITY	135
THE TOILET SEAT	136
MY NEUTERED DOG	137
MENSTRUAL PERIOD	138
LOVE AND WINE	139
IF YOU'RE GREEDY IT'S TRUE	140
A TEASE	141
SKINNY	142
G.A.S. (GRANDMOTHERS AGAINST SPEEDERS)	143
SUICIDE?	146
GOLDFISH	147
NEVER MIND	148
WHY I DON'T DO CROSSWORD PUZZLES	149
WHY PEOPLE COMMIT CRIMES	150
"WHERE HAVE YOU BEEN?!"	151
WHY I GOT IN TROUBLE AS A CHILD	152
WHEN THE TRUTH COMES OUT	153
A BETTER NEIGHBOR	154
OBSTACLES & PERCEPTION	155
THUNDERBIRD DREAMS	156
JESUS DRANK BEER	157
COFFEE SHOP CADENCE	158
THE LIFE, AN ACHE, AN ITCH	160

QUIBBLING TIMES	161
THE WINNER AND THE WHINER	162
CANDLE'S CLIME	163
HUMAN SHEEP	164
THE CIRCLE OF LIFE	165
I LEARN MORE ON SUNDAY MORNINGS	166
DISSOLVE	167
AT LAST MY FATHER IS WISE	168
LOVE'S CORNERSTONE	169
DÉJÀ VU	170
IN PRAISE OF NATURAL DISASTERS	171
ALL I AM IS ALL I KNOW	173
BECAUSE I LIVED	174
TWO LITTLE THINGS	175
THANK YOU	176
BRAINKEEPING	177
MEMORY'S COMPLEXION	178
LITTLE BOY, WITH KNAPSACK TIED	179
THE SUN ALSO RISES, BUT WHY?	181
SLICE OF LIFE	182
OUR LOVE, OUR LOVE	183
BLISS?	184
I GROW MORE LIKE MYSELF	185
MY EDEN'S AURA	186
EVERY DAY AT FIVE	189
X	190
THREE MORTAL VERSIONS	191
BIBLE AND BIG BANG	192
IN-LAWS	193
AN EPIC IN A SENTENCE	194
HEADS OR TAILS?	195
FALLING ASLEEP ON MY SOFA ON A SATURDAY AFTERNOON	196
QUEST EONS	197
PLUS SIGN	198
RUBBLE TROUBLE	200
THE MARROW OF MIRTH	201
PRINCESSES AND PEAS	202

STILLBIRTH	203
PERFECT CHOICE	206
THE SNAIL'S ANSWER	207
PROUD AS ONE	209
VINEGAR AND WINE	210
THE PERSUASION OF SANCTIMONY	212
THE SHAPE OF LOVE	213
LOVE IS . . .	214
MIDNIGHT STROLLS ON BACK-COUNTRY ROADS AND CARS THAT COME OUT OF NOWHERE	215
POSTCARDS FROM HELL	216
MY FRIENDS	218
CAFFEINE AND CONSCIENCE	219
FUMBLING WITH CHANGE: FOOTPRINTS ON THE WALL	220
NUTCRACKER	222
A DECORATED SOLDIER	223
ON THE HORIZON	225
BE THE AUTHOR OF YOUR LIFE	226
CLOSING VOYAGE	228
LIVE, LIVE, LIVE, LIVE	229
THE BLADE OF BIAS	230
MY DOG DOES NOT BLUSH	231
INSTANT KARMA	232
CONVERSATION CLOSED	233
COMET	234
THUNDER'S SONNET	235
A WOMAN'S WORK	236
AND YOU THOUGHT TRIGONOMETRY WAS HARD	237
A TALE TWICE TOLD	238
FREE YOUR MIND	239
WE SHOULD HAVE BEEN A-GIVING	240
UNDERSTANDING	241
DIGITAL MAN	242
SO LIKE CHILDREN ARE THE AGED	243
SAYDOBE	244
REVERSAL REHEARSAL	245
THE HANDS GO ROUND	246
A SELFISH MOTHER	247

WOODCHUCK	248
IF ONLY EARTH HAD A SPIN CYCLE	249
SHARING YOUR BLINDNESS	250
AT THE EDGE OF INNOCENCE	251
POLITICS AND RELIGION	252
THE RULES	253
HOLLOW WORDS	254
HISTORY	255
A JUMP FROM REASON	256
FOREVER YOUNG	257
HUNGER AND DEFEAT	258
DEATHLESS LOVE	259
RIGHTS	260
QUOD ERAT DEMONSTRANDUM	261
IN SPITE OF PLASTIC FLOWERS	262
BEFORE IT'S TOO LATE	263
AMADEUS	264
PASS SOON AWAY	265
REASON FOR REPENTANCE	266
NO CIRCLE SO SOUND	267
THRESHOLD	268
INSULT TO INJURY	269
REMEMBERING CHILDHOOD	270
DAMN THIS SNOW!	271
EMILY'S IN THE ATTIC	272
THE TOWN AN ETERNITY AWAY: A BOY ON A FARM	273
A MEAGER SEED	274
Y2K	275
O CHARLIE BOY	276
I'M IT	277
REGRETS	278
STRAPPED	279
HATEMONGERS	280
THE MEASURE OF SUCCESS	281
DEPARTED FLOWER	282
THE FINAL TOLL: A FAREWELL TO LIBERTY	283
JUST A THOUGHT. . .	284

BANISHED	285
BE STILL, LILY	286
PROMONTORY	287
FAINTING STEPS	288
THE TIME ON SOMEONE ELSE'S WATCH	289
TWO SONS	290
LAST CHRISTMAS	291
TON UPON TON UPON TON	293
AFTER A HOUSE OF CARDS	294
THE LAST COWBOY	295
HALF YES, HALF NO, HALF STAY, HALF GO	297
THE DEEPEST SUFFERING	298
THE CHASM	299
AMERICA, AMERICA	300
A POCKED ELLIPSE	302
KANSAS LOVES COMPANY	303
ACCOUNTABLE	304
APOCALYPTIC REVERSAL	305
FALLING APART	306
HARD HABITS TO BREAK	307
A UNIQUE FLOWER	309
A PARENT'S PRAYER FOR A CHILD SOLDIER	310
SHE SAID GOOD-BYE	311
BURN VICTIM	313
SEPARATION	314
POISONED SEEDS: THE WAIF, THE WHORE, THE SOCIETY	315
THOUGHT UPON SEEING A BAREFOOT BOY	316
DERAILED TRAIN OF THOUGHT	317
A VOICE FOR CHANGE	318
SLANT	319
SHADOWS AND AFRICAN AMERICANS	320
HOOKER	321
I KNOW THAT ONE	322
INTERLUDE FOR RELIGION	323
RECOVERING	324
I SEE THE SEA NO MORE	325
I HATE COLORS	326

AT THE CONVENTION OF PAST TYRANTS AND GENERALS	327
SWEET SACHET	328
WHAT SUBTERFUGE IS THIS, O HEART	329
RAPETURE	330
TEACH THE CHILDREN WELL	331
ZEBRAS IN THE ATTIC	332
ROTTEN MILK	333
DISGUSTED	334
THE CLOSING	335
ONE RACE: HUMAN	336
PACKS	337
FRUSTRATION	338
STARVING THE CROWS	339
SYLLABLE COUNTER	350
IRONY FINDS ME IN THE LIBRARY	351
SUICIDE: A PERMANENT SOLUTION TO A TEMPORARY PROBLEM	352
DIVORCE COURT	353
HELPLESS	354
VOYAGE	355
SHRINKING BACKYARD	356
THE MOURNING AFTER	357
JERK BLUES	358
DEATH	359
MONDAY MOURNING	360
GRANDPA'S HANDS	361
A CAROUSEL OF DAYS	362
A CASE FOR WILLN'T	363
A DEAD SOLDIER SPEAKS	364
A FLY FORETELLS OF WINTER	365
A FRIEND'S ATTENTION	366
A LITTLE MADNESS	367
A NEW WEIGHT-LOSS PROGRAM	368
A SEASIDE GIFT	369
A THIRD PARTY	370
A WOMAN'S CHOICE	372
AN ENEMY OUTRIGHT	374

AN EXAMPLE OF INARGUABLE LOGIC	375
AND THE PEOPLE	376
ANTICONFESSIONAL	377
ARGUMENT	378
AS A MAN SO LEAVES HIS YOUTH	379
POEM IN POEM	380
AS I WAS YOUNG	381
ASHES TO ASHES, DIAPERS TO DIAPERS	383
AT HER OWN HAND	384
ATTITUDE PLATITUDE	385
AUTUMNAL REVELATION	386
BECAUSE	387
BETWEEN THE LINES	388
BEYOND ICE	389
BIBLE SALES	390
BIRD FLU	391
BODY LANGUAGE	392
BUTTERFLY	393
BY SIGHT BUT NOT SOUND	394
CASTAWAYS	395
COLLATERAL DAMAGE	396
COLLISION	397
COMING BACK AS A BUG	398
CORPUS CALLOSUM	399
DEATH AT SEA	400
DEATH IN THE DESERT	401
DÉJÀ VU TWO	402
DISTRACTED BY A PRETTY WAITRESS	403
DONE	404
DRIVING WITH THE MAGIC MAN	405
DUTY	406
ECONOMICS 101: THE NEED TO EAT, AKA THE REASON DESIGNER SHIRTS EXIST	407
EGOISTS	408
ET TU	409
EXORCISING THE PAST	410
EZRA'S ACROSTIC	411
FAMILY REUNION	412

FATHER TIME	414
FEAR	415
FEAST OR FAMINE	416
FIFTEEN EPIGRAMS FOR NO ONE IN PARTICULAR	417
FIST	420
FLUX	421
FOUR, NOT FIVE	422
FREE FALLING	423
FROM A BOAT UPON THE GREEN	425
FROM THE TOP	426
GIFTS FOR A MURDERER	427
GIVING UP	428
HAIKU SUNSET	429
HAPPINESS	430
HE WHO ADMITS WHEN HE IS WRONG IS WISE	431
HIGGLEDY-PIGGLEDY	432
HOW A BOY BECAME A POET	433
I AM NOT THE POET	435
I BELIEVE	436
"I'LL BE RIGHT BACK"	438
I.R.S. AUDIT	439
IN PRAISE OF NUMBER ONE	440
INERTIA	442
FIRESIDE WINE	443
JE NE SAIS QUOI NI QUAND	444
KINDNESS	445
LAST RIDE	446
LATE DECEMBER DAYDREAM	447
LAWYERVILLE	448
LESSONS	450
LIES	451
LIVING IN THE PAST	452
LONGING	453
LOST SHEPHERDS	454
LOVE LETTER FROM A LAWYER	455
MARRIAGE	457
MAYBE I COULD MAKE A MILLION	458

MERRIMENT IN THE DOSE	459
MISSING	461
MISTAKE REALIZED AT EIGHTEEN	462
MY OWN RELIGION	463
NAMES	464
NEVER TEST THE DEPTH OF WATER WITH BOTH FEET	465
NOAH	467
NOTHING MADE CAN LAST, NOTHING WROUGHT CAN STAY	470
NOW AS AGO	471
ODYSSEY OF THE ANT	472
OF ALL THE POEMS I HAVE WRITTEN, THIS IS PERHAPS THE ONE WITH THE LONGEST TITLE	474
OF COMPLICATIONS FROM A FALL	475
OH, THE BOOKS I OWN BUT HAVEN'T READ	476
ON WHAT'S ABOUT TO HAPPEN NEXT	477
ORDER	478
PEACHY	479
PEARLS BEFORE SWINE	480
PENCILS, PENS, PAPER	481
PERSPECTIVE	483
PI	484
POET'S BLOCK	485
PORK CHOPS	486
PREPOSITIONS ARE WORDS YOU SHOULDN'T END SENTENCES WITH	487
RACCOON	488
RAIL-SPLITTER	489
READING THE DEAD POETS	490
REARVIEW NAP	491
RICHARD CORY'S BROTHER	492
RUSH-HOUR DREAMS	493
SAVE THAT BEAST CALLED MAN	494
SCHOOL OF HARD KNOCKS	495
SEA-WINE SESTINA	496
SERENDIPITY	498
SHE LOVED NOT ME BUT MY MONEY	499
SHOUT	500
SILVER LINING	501

SNOWGLOBE	502
SPLIT DECISION	503
STEALING EMILY	504
STONE WISDOM	507
STONES WE'VE THROWN	508
T.G.I.F.	509
TEATIME DAYDREAM	510
TEST	511
THE ANIMALS SPEAK OF MAN	513
THE AUTHOR'S VISIT	514
THE BARN	517
THE BEAUTIFUL, MERCILESS LADY	519
THE CARDINAL AND THE WORM	521
THE CORD	522
THE DIMINISHED PUPIL	523
THE GAMBLER'S LAMENT	524
THE GRASS UPON THE BATTLEFIELD	525
THE INCOMPLETE WORKS, PLEASE	526
THE MAGIC WORD	527
THE ONLY WAY I'LL GET TO HEAVEN	528
THE PUBLISHER WANTS	529
THE PARADOX OF SOCKS	530
THE QUIET MUSIC OF MADNESS	531
THE RIGHT WAY TO HOLD A FORK	532
THE SIX RESTRAINTS	533
THE THIRD CANDIDATE	535
THE TIGHTROPE OF REGRET	536
THE TRUTH ABOUT THE PAST	537
THE VERY END	538
THIS IS LIKE TALKING TO MY WIFE	539
TO NEW ENGLAND FROM ENGLAND	540
TOO MUCH SAKI	541
TWENTY-FIRST-CENTURY ANTS	542
UPON RETURNING	543
USED GOODS	544
VENI, VIDI, VEGGIE	545
VERSE SCIOLTI DA RIMA	546

VITA BREVIS	547
W.B.	548
WAITING	549
WALKING THE DOG	550
WAR'S OTTAVA RIMA	551
WE TWO LONELY FOOLS	552
WEEP FOR ME NO MORE	553
WHAT DOES HUMAN SAY?	554
WHAT THE EARTH IS WORTH	555
WHEN I AM DEAD	556
WHEN SHE'S ONLY BEAUTIFUL	557
WHEN TO REST WE LAY THE WORLD'S SWAY	558
DEATH ON PARSON'S POND	559
WORDS OF INSPIRATION FROM A SOAP OPERA STAR	560
X SPEAKS	561
CONSCIENCE	562
TRUST	563
THE LAZARUS EFFECT	564
A POEM WRITTEN IN THREE-LETTER WORDS BEGINNING WITH O	566
YOU, ROBERT FROST	567
CLOSING ILLNESS	568
A BEGINNER'S GUIDE TO CREATING A RELIGION	569
I LIKE SHORT POEMS BEST	570
IF I LIVE TO SEE TOMORROW	571
EVOLUTIUON, BABY!	572
AFTER PANGAEA	573
PACKING THE POETS	574
BROKEN GLASS	575
TODAY'S POETRY	576
ALMOST	577
ONANISTIC INTERLUDE	578
ZERO TO YOU IN TEN SECONDS	580
ARMS AND LEGS	581
SPACE	582
BOUYS	583
THE LAST LAUGH	584
INDEX OF TITLES AND FIRST LINES	587

ANTHOLOGY
—of—
ONE

1990-2007
Collected Poems of J.L. Hittle

THE BEGINNING

Once was when,
Time forgotten now,
Used to be
Never was.

I ALONE

A meticulous man was he,
Replete in his expectancy,
And swift with a corrective hand
For me, his wayward prodigy,

Whenever I did fail to band
The way of his accustomed brand
With my innate and callow needs,
To him so often out of hand.

No forced will will a flower heed,
But pine instead to be a weed,
And better off than that which grows
Arrested as a shaded seed.

A second self, a child, suppose,
As the reflection of your pose,
Is as two where but one may grow,
And I alone am proof to show.

A WORD WITHHELD

A word withheld works a wonder
Where utterance denies:
A gem shines brightest when concealed
From yet contented eyes.

He is thunder without lightning
Who sits and stupefies,
Whose hand lies with its cards revealed;
His sleeve without surprise.

A FATHER IS TOLD THAT HIS SON IS DEAD, AND THEN TOLD HE IS THE WRONG FATHER

It is how the fish cannot understand
what the hell just happened,
why it's lying on the deck of a boat
staring up into a blurry sky
with its one alarmed eye,
a stinging in its mouth as it tries
to swim through the air but cannot
even right its oval-shaped body
on the planks it flounders against,
slapping its head repeatedly until
it reaches a whole new state of dizzy
and cannot understand why it,
all of sudden, cannot breath—
and then, back in the stream, it can.

A GUY SAYS TO ME

that he likes my shoes

so I start to tell him
where I got them

but he stops me and says

I didn't say I wanted a pair
I just said I liked them

to this day
no one in my book has gone
from nice guy to asshole
any faster

with the possible
exception of the jerk
who bought the shoes
in the first place

A RENTAL TRUCK FILLED WITH FERTILIZER

in an age where T-shirts are billboards
and car bumpers dispense political advice
and rear windows college affiliations
in an attempt to show the whole damn world
just how fucking smart the owners are
in an age of black and white and white and black
so black and so white and so wrong and so right
in an age where nobody really knows squat
about anything that really matters anyway
I say it's exactly the same as yesterday
and it's exactly the same as it'll be tomorrow
we're gonna go on screwing this up
until we evolve into something better

A THREE-LEGGED DOG NAMED HOOVER

A three-legged dog named Hoover taught me
that there are two types of handicapped people:
Those with a handicap and those who are a handicap.
Both have disabilities, but only one lives as if he does.

Hoover hopped better than any kangaroo I've ever seen.
He didn't want a handicap, and so, in his mind,
he didn't have one.
He lived as though he had six legs.

People could learn a lot from a three-legged dog named Hoover.

A YOUNG PRESIDENT

Much time passed.
A conscientious man was troubled.
He had never done this before—
wasn't sure he wanted to do it now.

She was a young American,
tall and sturdy,
moved with athleticism,
her gestures larger than necessary.

But there was a soft insistence about her,
a subtle gravity that could not be denied—
would not be denied.
"Come with me," was all she said.

He did, and was never the same again.

I HAD OTHER PLANS FOR MY LIFE

I had other plans for my life, you know. But things rarely if ever go just as I planned. It's difficult to imagine that a single drop of rain can alter the course of my existence, but it can. Forget the big and glaring decisions I've made, those are easy to recognize. It's the noise that startled me and kept me on the sidewalk just long enough to avoid stepping in front of a speeding car; it's the time I was in the bathroom when co-workers collected money for the lottery ticket that won; it's the time I stopped to tie my shoe and in so doing missed the bus, which kept me another thirty minutes in the rain, the day I met you on my ride home; it's the day we both called in sick because neither of us felt like working, the day our son was conceived, the day I knew I wanted to spend the rest of my life with you. It's these moments and a million others just like them—the kind you don't give a second thought—that have changed and shaped my life. It's the time that I took to write these lines that has prevented me from doing something else. It's the time that I took to write these lines that has changed my life forever.

THE SPACES BETWEEN

The swashbucklers are rarely if ever happy.
The rabble-rousers seek attention for their discord—
Not for their dress or any other outward symptom,
But for their lack of self, their discord within.
The arrogant shrink behind their masks of pomp,
Curl up in their self-made corners of inferiority
And weep without impunity for their insolence.
The know-it-alls dismiss the wisdom of others
For fear of being outshone or outwitted;
And then, when they can, change their stories
Altogether—recounting instead of recanting.
The spaces between people and reality are filled
With lenses fashioned to bend, shift, and blur the truth—
As distorted to those looking out as to those looking in.

LITTLE PINK COAT

In a place where sterility teeters
on the brink of disease,
a hallway in a hospital,
I pass a man clutching
a small pink coat against his chest.
When our eyes meet
I can see the welling of his tears,
and I cannot look at him.

Paces past
I hear a loud and painful scream.
I turn to see him on his knees,
his face stuffed deep into the little pink coat,
a doctor's hand upon his shoulder.

Later that night
I argue with my wife
over our checking account.
Mid-sentence
I remember the man
with the little pink coat,
his sense of helplessness amplified
by his fatherly instinct
to protect his little girl.

I am angry beyond anger.
What asses we are!

BONE UPON BONE

When some excavator finds my bones
He will not know how once they flew
As quick up stairs as down.
He will not know the size of the heart
That filled the cage he sees right through,
Nor how blue the eyes
That beheld from now-hollow sockets
The wonder of their first everything.
He will not have the first idea of any idea
That filled the brain that filled the skull
He holds in his not-long-fleshed fingers.
But perhaps he will realize that
His fingers are not long fleshed,
And then, perhaps, he will leave me to my own,
As each of us is left: bone upon bone.

CALLING TO ARTHUR

Arthur, my fifty-two-pound beagle,
who lives to eat, sleep, and howl,
lies In the doorway of my bedroom.

I call to him . . .

He lifts his head and looks at me,
his eyes as heavy as the sandman's sack.
"C'mon on, Art! C'mere, boy!"

He exhales sharply through his nose,
plops his head on the carpet,
and goes back to sleep.

He always listens this way.

"Good boy, Arthur. Good boy."

CARNIVAL SEVENTEEN

In cotton-candy air
Under Ferris-wheel skies,
She with roller-coaster curves
And I a ticket to ride . . .

The hammer was a sword,
The baseball was a lance,
The teddy bear a dragon,
And a dollar for each chance.

CARPE DIEM
(a toast)

Who can tell us how we should live?
Who can say the way it should be?
What does giving a judgment give
When to all what shall be shall be?

Too near cliché we close our ears
When others say that life is short—
Aye, we say it ourselves with tears
Yet wish a day away like sport.

And still the past and future lie
Divided by a golden rift:
The now though which we often fly
Too fast upon its winged gift.

Today is here, upon us now,
And it shall never come anew,
So raise a cup with me and vow
To seize each day your whole life through!

CORN

what's not real
what's not necessary
the homespun theories of thinking man
our spaceship rumbling through darkness
the indigestible corn floating in the bowl
the tick trying to burrow its way under my skin
the feces and the flies and the famine
oh it's a wonderful life
and the lifelong smoker is suing
and the girl with the fake boobs is suing
and I'm suing too
I want my money back

"YOU LOOK JUST LIKE YOUR FATHER"

We used to have the best discussions, my father and I. I would say: "A strong government relies on the acquiescence of its subject people." And he would say: "History shows us that insurrection—an utter lack of acquiescence—has, at times, created stronger governments. The United States is a prime example." "True enough," I would say. "After the insurrection and the establishment of a new government, however, the acquiescence of the subject people is still crucial to the new government's success." "Good point," he would say, nodding his head in contemplation. And so it was, point and counterpoint, example and counterexample, ruminating on the ideas we shared. Never arguing but learning from one another, growing in likeness, father and son.

DEATH BY A THOUSAND CUTS

silence broken
a stone through a pane
forgettable words falling like clichés
from the lips of someone with no truth
"never again, never again"
again and again forgiveness kills
slowly, like the time before, doubling into less
bleeding into the gluttony of the spineless
no ends, only beginnings
only more
only more and more and more

DESCRIBING A RAINBOW TO A BLIND MAN

What if I could paint a picture with words so keen
that I could make color, size, and shape be seen?
To say the sun looks like orange juice tastes,
that polka dots appear the feel of an unshaven face,
that blue is ice and red is fire,
that water is lower and wind is higher,
that pins and needles are the sight of stars,
that comets appear the sound of passing cars,
that the ocean looks bigger than a sneeze,
that opera sounds like the shape of trees,
that being drunk looks like a clown,
and that frogs appear just as they sound—
then, maybe then, a rainbow can
be more than a word to a sightless man.

DIFFERENCE QUANTIFIED

The dirt of the day collects beneath my nails. The twentieth century has come and gone. There are now six billion people on the planet. If I live to eighty I will have lived for more than forty-two million seconds.

Collectively, there are more than two hundred thousand eighty-year-old lives lived every day. There is a lifetime in every second. I have forty-two million of them.

Each day throws itself upon me. Can I make a difference in my life? Can I make a difference in a day? My friend, I can make a difference in a second!

DIVINITY

The world is
indifferent to my words
and goes on killing.

To capture horror
without surrendering
is to grow stronger.

Sometimes it is better
to be the victim
than the perpetrator.

To become mighty
is to succumb to
the pyrite of the mighty.

To be vulnerable
through acceptance
is divine.

CONSIDERING HE WAS SUPPOSED TO BE IN PRISON

Considering he was supposed to be in prison by the time he was eighteen, so his father had predicted time and time again (reverse psychology to the nth degree), he considered himself successful at thirty-one, taking stock one evening from the comfort of his home. He had a good job and a steady income. He had a beautiful and loving wife. He drove a nice car. He had a couple of good friends. Still, in spite of his success, he felt unfulfilled and hollow, like an oyster with a pearl but no meat. It wasn't the approbation of his father, that had been given, and his mother had always believed that he would succeed. He seemed to lack meaning and purpose, both of which had been embodied in his pursuit of success, or so he thought. But now he sat on the couch of his success, watched the television of his success, walked on the carpet of his success, and drank the wine of his success. He was inflated by the sheer space of his success, a vast chasm forged by the torrent of what he now felt were trivial pursuits. What, then, was missing? What did he lack? What was it that he could possibly attain that would fulfill him? On that evening, while the world rolled toward yet another day, he wondered if he would ever have the gift of happiness, a gift he knew could only come from himself. He arose, kissed his wife goodnight, and went to bed hopeful.

ECHOES OF EMILY

I've read and re-read every word.
I've loitered on her pages long.
I've smiled when the music heard
Caused pause to hear the poet's song.

I never heard her state her choice—
She passed before I could be—
Yet certain am I of her voice
As though tonight she sang to me.

EXPLOITED TO FEEL LOVED

So this stray dog is your new friend,
And wherever you go he follows?
Not to be rude but when he looks at your food
He licks his chops and swallows.

HALF?

Has anyone seen my love,
My little flicka who
Stood upon this altar
But vanished with "I do"?

And who is this imposter
Standing 'fore me now,
This shadow of resemblance,
This litigating cow?

Give me back the giddy knee
I had walking down the aisle!
And take away this newfound hate
For that cat with the Cheshire smile!

FOOLS' FRIENDS

My purse strings stung
into my hands
the weight of gold
of lesser brands—

and friends had I
from far and near
ever ready
to lend an ear—

but ever with
averted eyes
upon the pyrite
of my prize.

But now I sit,
my secret told,
without a friend
but my fools' gold.

And sure am I
my heart will heal
once I find
a friend who's real.

GIFTS YOU CAN'T BUY

When the magic of Christmas is a half-off sale
at your favorite department store;
when giving is going through the motions
that you've been through before;
when your idea of holiday cheer
is a day from the maddening crowd;
when Yule swings in like a fist to your chin
and hangs over your head like a cloud—
try to remember each deep December
there are soldiers not coming home;
there are children dying and mothers crying
and homeless who know not where to roam—
then perhaps you'll know what it's like to go
without while the shoppers fly by;
perhaps you'll feel a pain that can't heal
with gifts you go out and buy.

MY PARTICLES WILL COALESCE

My particles will coalesce into more or less than I am today long after I as you know me am gone. So comes the day I cannot mark yet know waits for me precisely upon the tick I am no longer, the day that takes me to where some stay and some go, the day I become a memory instead of a rising and a setting. (Oh, how we begin so small with so little but are so big and with so much!) If I could have recognized not only that the world turns into our diminishment, but that it simultaneously pulls us with its gravity into its potential and its wonder, then perhaps I could have marked each moment and each breath as a singular gift, appreciated fully the awesome power that lay before me moment upon moment. It is only now that the twilight comes so quickly upon the last and the last that I pause as in hope to save but one forever in this vast landscape that has turned before me like a motion picture, the first reel playing while the second records and captures, their capacity spinning into great speculation, into a gamble of my leisure and my ease. I know that soon the credits roll and the camera turns to the spot where I left my favorite shoes powerless to tie themselves, powerless to walk on their own.

HAPPY BIRTHDAY, ROOM 202

She lay withered
by years too many to count,
the woman they called "Room 202."

Ninety pounds of wrinkles and failing organs,
of chins and gnarls and macaroni nails,
of scribbled hair and the odor of unbathed skin:
the heavy weight of reduction.

Once the man on the nightstand
gazed at her in wonder;
the children in her locket
suckled for survival
but now are grown and gone.
She was once someone
remembered, loved, adored.

But today no callers come and no candles count.
Room 202 is still, yet the sun still shines.
And she, too, had forgotten, I thought,
save the rain in her cataract sky.

I DIE

My name has DIE in it.
Why does my name have DIE in it?
The J and O are fine,
It's the D and I and E—
The DIE that concerns me.

I suppose die is in everyone's name.

I DOUBT

Dawn by the river.
The priest holds me under
a little too long.
I choke on his religion
and spit it back into the water.
He apologizes
and asks if I would like to do it over.
I tell him that I am all set.

On my way home,
water sloshing in my shoes,
gospel burning in my lungs,
past bums huddled in shadows
cast by marble pillars,
past a dead cat
wearing a collar and a bell,
past this reality and that,
I leave footprints on the concrete.

And just above the horizon
I see perfect beams splayed
out through the parting clouds
like fingers to open hands.
I thirst like a desert.
I go to drink but find it
difficult to swallow.

I ENVY

A sun unto itself,
I envy the falltime birch,
its red and golden amulets
falling to winter's lurch

until there stands a moon
harvested of light,
its leafless arms to bear
the heft of winter's white:

I envy for again it's green
and I but once naive;
I envy for its light returns
while for youth I grieve;

I envy for again it shines
its face adorned anew;
I envy for my leaves have yellowed
and never shall renew.

I FORGET

The sun was . . .
well, I'm sure the sun was like anything.
And the trees that day were . . .
well, to be honest,
I don't recall how the trees were,
or even if there were trees.
But let me tell you of the birds.
Oh, the birds. . . let me see . . . the birds—
hell! I don't remember if there were birds.
If there were, then there were trees, I'm sure.
The truth is I don't remember
if there were trees or birds,
or whether it was day or night.
But thank you for holding my hand
while we walked in the park . . .
It was the park, wasn't it?

I GRIEVE

the naked birches stand
haphazard on the strand
like veins of gray rain
on a winter windowpane
of forgotten summer sand

in one a gull takes ease
from the break of the sea's
fervor and thirst which at first
deflate but then burst
as with great hate on the keys

in another a nest
which at once held the breast
and the voice and the wing
of so brief a fledgling
rests as vacant as my chest

and the lonely gull I spy
through this gray pane's eye
cries as I with a moan
for our fledglings have flown
to the dark side of the sky

I HAVE LEARNED

I have walked beyond the city lights and have learned more in silence than in a classroom.

I have looked over my shoulder at yesterday and have learned that now is all I have.

I have listened to the theories of scholars and sages and priests and have learned that what I believe is what matters most.

I have studied history and have learned that it cannot teach me about tomorrow.

I have squandered opportunities and ruined relationships and have learned a greater appreciation for them both.

I have been ill and have lost others to illness and have learned that health is more precious than wealth.

I have learned that I have total control and no control, that I am at once mighty and meek, significant and insignificant, and so is everyone else.

I have learned that giving is the greatest gift of all.

I have learned to always learn; it is the only way to live.

I HOPE

May something always go unsolved,
May some longing go unsatisfied
And some question unanswered.
May we never know everything.
Then tomorrow there is hope.

THE HUNGER OF HOPE

Surely there is something more worthwhile than hope?
Tomorrow taunts me from its ageless horizon:
"Things will change, everything will get better."
So I cling to hope like some frightened child
wrapped around its mother's leg, holding on
for dear life to be spared from the monster,
but upon waking realize that I have been devoured.

I LEARN

The midday sun,
hot like a branding iron,
stamps its oppressive
feet on my skull
until my mind begins to boil
and I need refuge
from its inferno.

In the shade
I realize the same sun
that drove me to shelter
casts a cool and forgiving
shadow of relief
over my body,
like a salve soothing my burns.

I LIKE THIS POEM

I don't know if you'll like this poem,
but I do.
Truth is, I really don't care.
Well, I mean, I care,
but not about whether or not you'll like this poem.
"What is he trying to say?" you might ask
after reading this poem.
And to that I would have to say that
you'll need to read between the lines.
Read it over, especially the part about
my not caring if you'll like this poem.
"Is this really even a poem?" you might wonder.
Oh, I think it is, and what's more
I think you're really going to like it. Yes.
In fact, I am sure you will.
I do.

HE DREAMED OF RISING IN A NEW YORK FLAT

He dreamed of rising in a New York flat to the Sunday Times' crossword puzzle, the dusty Manhattan sunlight beaming in over a rich leather ottoman, next to which, on a marble-topped table, sat a cup of coffee and a pen. He dreamed while he reclined in the Sunday morning sunlight that the answers he knew from the first to the last clue flowed from his pen in quick succession, halted only briefly for an intermittent sip of coffee. And because this was a dream, the coffee never cooled or lowered in his cup, its steam kept rising to its invisible six-inch ceiling, where it disappeared among the particles of light, among the words of articles he couldn't see to read, words he had no desire to read. And now, with the crossword finished—flawlessly—he paused to inhale his satisfaction, to let it fill his lungs completely before he shared it with the room. And then, after a moment in contemplation, in steam, blurred words and particles of light, he turned the page to find a new puzzle in his never-ending paper of puzzles.

I MIGHT

The dust of a millennium
collects on the wordless pages
of a book called Tomorrow.
The cobwebs in the corners
of forgotten aspirations,
of neglected ambitions,
collect the hope of time,
the solution of tomorrow.
Dreams that remain dreams
dangle motionless from gossamers
above a floor that shatters
all that falls upon it.
The wind outside rattles
the portal to tomorrow.
I approach with care,
work the latch from its rust,
take hold of the dusty knob,
and will turn it, perhaps, tomorrow.

IF I WERE BLACK

If I were black
I would show only my palms
to the man with the job to fill.

If I were black
I would show only my teeth
to the man asking if I am hungry.

If I were black
I would show only my soles
to the man fitting me for shoes.

If I were black
I would show only my mind
to the person asking the question.

If I were black
I would show only my faith
to the preacher asking my religion.

If I were black
I would show only my reluctance
to the cop asking me to step from the car.

If I were black, who could blame me?

I THIRST

To close my eyes for death
would surely bring more light
than midday in your absence.
You are the sun's sun,
and he rises in my eyes
only because I know you.
To want you
is to thirst upon the sea.
To wish you into my arms
is to know eternity.
To seek you
is to row but one oar,
and in return step within
the tracks I laid before.
You are every breath and every beat;
the whole world round beneath my feet.
You are my want of heaven when away.
Alas, you too are hell each vacant day.

WORDS LABEL UNTIL THEY OFFEND

Words label until they offend—or, more specifically, until we find them offensive (words in and of themselves are powerless to offend, after all, they are merely letters arranged into syllables and sounds). Yes, words label until they offend, so we change them into new words—less offensive, less derogatory words, words that haven't yet had time to become pointed, stigmatic, derisive or belittling. It is we who make and take exception, we, the inventors of language who label for ease of recognition, and in so doing find that we have defined and otherwise classified in broad strokes whole groups of these, them, and those. Of course, it is only the labels we use for ourselves in which we find offense. The dichotomy of those with language—to be simultaneously exclusive and included—is a tug of war between two poles to which our hands are nailed. We will never be happy with what others call us; never happy with what we call ourselves.

I, PRONOUN

This, that, these and those—
demonstrative pronouns standing for toes.
You can read but can't take a look—
they stand for toes on either foot.
Write without and redundancy shows—
tough to read as to stand without toes.

HOW SWEET THE CRUST

How sweet the crust stolen from the cooling pie;
How bright the gem hidden from the wanting eye;
How common the secret once kept but now shared;
How boring the boy who does all he is dared;
How spoiled the beauty when exposed from the veil;
How stabbing the teeth cloaked by wag in the tail;
How small the mountain in the distance we see;
How pretty the thistle that stings like a bee;
How perfect the present still wrapped in ribbon;
How unvalued the love missed when not given;
Oh, things are often not at all as they seem;
We live as we wish but then wake from the dream:
How sweet the crust stolen from the cooling pie,
Which later, when served, becomes salty and dry.

INNOCENCE LOST

Clouds have become clouds:
Horses I once saw are dead—
Saddled, enshrouded.

INNOCENCE LOST
(expanded version)

With age,
theirs and mine,
the clouds thin.
The horses I once made of their shapes
have become as shapeless as time,
theirs and mine.

Sad, sad age has dulled my eyes,
covered them with accountable shrouds,
killed the horses of my skies,
and turned the clouds to clouds.

THE HUNGRY WAVES

How petty I feel at the sea,
How powerless it renders me
Whenever I behold the waves
Consume themselves then rise again:
A liquid phoenix stratagem:

Their white fangs gnashing on the sand,
Feeding faces with bubbling hands
Until the moon takes up their dish
And they reluctantly retreat
To muster up new shores to eat.

See at once a wolf and a sheep,
Both at once awake and asleep.
They have power without power,
In every part and in the whole:
They have a soul without a soul.

Behold how they swell as they ride
Upon the backbone of the tide!
How not one is spent when it breaks
But swallowed whole by its own wake
And turned inward for its own sake!

See how they give nothing for good
But loan instead their misty hood
To a thirsty sun that gathers
It up like an aerial shroud,
Paints it white and creates a cloud;

A downy purse in which to hold
The treasure of earth's liquid gold

But in a temporary home,
For soon each greedy cloud does burst
And spill out the spoils of its thirst

In droplets of miniature waves
Upon the earth, which in turn saves
Each upon each until they reach
A measure strong enough to flow.
Then again, as eons ago,

They march a trickled cadence down,
Like soldiers coming back to town
Long after they were marched away,
Into the body they will be:
The awaiting arms of the sea.

They are a part, they are the whole,
Impartible from swell to shoal,
Displaced but temporarily
By oars and ships and swimming things,
They join in what their joining brings.

And not one drop upon this earth
Is lesser than the lesser's worth;
All have been and will be again—
Each puddle, each river, each lake,
Every fog and dew and snowflake—

What once and once forever gave,
Never collecting one to save,
Resurrected as from the grave—
Again, again, again a wave!
A wave, a wave, a hungry wave!

A DAY'S WORTH OF SNIPPETS

The faces of children are so familiar
that we do not feel like voyeurs
when we watch them.
But all too soon,
I cannot say exactly when,
they bear little resemblance
to our green, green memories,
and we avert our eyes
as if in shame when caught watching
what we have become,
although, as for that,
I cannot say exactly why.

As if on purpose
The oak bends into the yard.
I swap rake for axe.

His inimitable voice—
not its sound but its sense—
muted by a cacophony
of medical equipment,
a doctor's pondered prognosis,
a racing mind.
And like a child who talks
above the answer to his question,
I heard nothing.
I did not want to hear.

My hero lay on bleach-white sheets
and heavily on my heart.
My everything reduced

to speculation.
An ocean in a saltshaker.
An oak tree turned to a toothpick.
A tow truck towed.

To shine brings rapt attention to a polished skill,
but jealousy ensues when others have but will.

I put it in, I take it out.
I put it in, I take it out.
Is it better with
or better without?
Should it stay
or should it go?
Truth is I really don't know.
Damn commas!

The malice of the jealous with their voodoo wishes . . .

To be needed is the greatest power one has over another,
as the planet relies on sun and rain; the baby on its mother:

Power has he with others' dependence
for knowledge he possesses,
and to never fully fulfill their needs
keeps them in his dresses.

Wisdom is a second sun illuminating the way to a world worth having.

People have lost the gift of solitude.
It seems no one knows how to be alone,
entertain himself, or occupy his time with

his own worthwhile pursuits.
Instead, people complain in their whinny little voices:
"I'm bored. There's nothing to do."
And to fill the absence,
the self-imposed void,
the awkward silence,
mighty malls rise up from parking lots,
movie theaters spread like plagues,
their pimply-faced employees pushing
overpriced popcorn and name-brand cola
to a glassy-eyed nation of charge card holders.

To catch a butterfly in a mirror . . .
She was as fragile as a snowflake with low self-esteem.

SQUIRREL INDECISION

The squirrel is always crossing the road.
You'd think he'd be better at it by now.
You'd think he'd heed the carnage of his
indecisive brother's body flattened
by a steel-belted radial in a series of diminishing thuds.
But no, here he squirts again across the road.
And here I come, my car's pistons poised to pulverize.
He darts, and I think that at his pace he will make it easily.
But then he stops, and I can't believe it.
Is he stupid?
Is he some sort of Kamikaze squirrel on a suicide mission?
I cover the brake pedal and can almost hear him thinking:
"Perhaps I should turn back? No, I can make it.
Oh, shit! What should I do?"
"He'll move," I say to myself. But then I'm not so sure.
I slam on my brakes, and as my car swerves to avoid
the bushy-tailed rodent, the puffy-cheeked varmint,
I curse the squirrel, I curse its squirrel indecision.

I IMAGINE

I imagine in this concrete world
that the dirt of the day collecting
beneath my nails is the bed of folly.
I imagine that most of my pursuits,
like paychecks waged on lotteries,
yield to a diminishing spiral of time.
And I imagine it is the same
for everyone in every corner:
love is the only thing worth having.
Omnia vincit amor.

IN VINO VERITAS

There is truth in wine,
and so on her third glass
she told me that my suspicions were true.

I did not ask his name;
it would not have made a difference,
and It would not have brought her back.

In an instant I knew
that I would never see her again.
And like wine, there is truth in sorrow.

IN LINE AT THE GROCERY STORE

I stop sweating,
my skin blisters,
my lips crack, and
the blood hardens
and cracks again.
The water evaporates
before I can swallow.
The dog at my side
continues to chase
its tail in a circle.
I bury myself in
the sand for fear that
the vultures will eat
me. I expect no change.

JOB SECURITY

I would say he was around seventy,
the hunched man, the gaunt and wrinkled man
shuffling along in his city-issued orange vest,
picking up cigarette butts and dropping them one by one
from his mechanical claw into the garbage bag he held,
stopping every few feet or so to drag from his own,
and then, finally, dropping it and turning it into the walk
with the sole of his shoe, leaving it there, and moving on.

JANUARY 1, 2001

So here it is, the long-awaited
and much-hyped millennium:
the next measure of mankind.
1000 long-short years of us again
doing whatever it is we do.
And here I sit, poised at my keyboard,
ready to pounce, ready to say
something amazing, something
completely original and insightful,
but it's Monday, and you know Mondays.
Well, apparently they're the same
here in the new millennium,
because here I sit with the preceding
words having said nothing . . . nothing . . .
nothing millenniumesque, nothing
unlike anything I said yesterday
or the day before or the day before.
Perhaps I'll have to wait until tomorrow
to be filled with the wisdom that everyone
here in the third millennium
since we started counting
must surely have.
I do hope it comes soon, though,
at least before the fourth—
I'm certain I won't last that long.

MAGNUM OPUS

The wherewithal of a mother
is a work singular of all;
no musician or like other
can perform an order so tall.
The journeywork of the unsung
giver is grander than the stars;
the wishes of motherless young
fade like fireflies in airless jars.

MAGGOTS

They have eaten the bread of affliction,
Toasted and buttered and jellied up sweet:
The sugar-coated pill of addiction
That keeps them feeding on bitter deceit.

(How the promise of life eternal sings!)

And what goes against their better judgment,
Their plates full of penance and deference,
They weave right into the eye of the truth
Until they cannot see the difference.

(There must be angels if maggots grow wings!)

NONE OF THIS IS TRUE

Ever feel like it's all about you,
like all the other people in the world are extras,
actors put here to play some role in the story of *your* life?
Guess what, pal? You're right, they are.
Don't doubt yourself.
Ever walk into a store and just know that
the people behind the counter are talking about *you*?
Well, you're right again, friend, they are.
Ever wonder if it's all just one big conspiracy?
Of course it is! You know it is, man.
How about the woman who shoots you
a curious smile? She's up to something, right?
You better believe it, buddy.
She probably forgot her line or something.
It's all about you, baby, all about you.
Don't you forget it, you idiot!

MY HEART, MY HEAT, MY WONDER

It retracts like memory aged,
this feeling of vitality and summer lust
to which I have given wholly
my heart, my heat, my wonder.

I cannot say why it steals my senses
and then gives them back
spent like a breathless runner
who will never see the ribbon cut.

Again the foliage fills and falls
to the chestbeats of a cage
through which a heart longs
for an eternal summer.

Oh, everything dies,
and still the heart hopes and pines.
How beautiful it is to desire
life forever.

NERO'S ANACOLUTHON

If I fiddle while Rome burns,
Rome will burn whether I fiddle or not.
Perhaps I'll fiddle for rhetorical effect,
Effectively fiddling till it's too hot.
I shouldn't have played with the fire,
Peter and Paul warned me as well,
Something to do with eternal damnation
In a nether world they called hell.

PARADISE

There's a flower in a meadow
trampled by a hoof;
there's a butterfly in a web
atop a temple roof;
there's a spider in a faucet
frozen into ice;
there's a vulture in a desert
its own sacrifice:
and this, all this, is paradise.

OUT OF LIFE ITSELF

We are good at finding little truths
to persuade our better judgment into silence,
some little sake to let us live as we wish:
without the backlash of our conscience.
And all that doesn't suit us we ignore,
discredit or despise until it eats us up,
because we really can't ignore a thing.
We are great pretenders and great cheaters.
But eventually, if we're lucky, we open our eyes
and cannot deny the way things really are.
We learn that we have only been fooling ourselves,
cheating ourselves out of reality, out of life itself.

PUT A CORK IN IT

The grapes of future hangovers hang in the California sun, their thin skins stretched smooth and tight by the meat and the might of their insides. Like pregnant teenagers, their hopes swell, their tomorrows seem bright. But the weight of their lives soon grows too heavy for their umbilical vines to carry. The months reveal reality. Tomorrow comes and squashes yesterday's future. Some shrivel in the sun. Some split. Some spill. The world drinks its fill. The headaches begin.

RELICS

The relics of yesterday's wisdom lie in shards,
remnants of what was gospel and held as truth—
the way things were.

Today's scholars piece it all together,
gathering the evidence and weighing its validity,
their modern sciences disproving ancient theories,
debunking old ideas,
exposing fallacies.

Tomorrow's scholars will arrive with new ideas and new sciences
to collect our relics, dust them off, and have a good laugh, too.

WE ALL FALL DEAD

We sang "ring around the rosy,
pocket full of posy,"
unwittingly hearkening The Plague.
And slowly we learned as it turned
that not all at all is rosy
upon this stage.

PLOUGHSHARES

Until young men the world over refuse to die because old men cannot think will there be peace.

Cut up every battleship,
Dismantle every plane,
Turn missiles into planters,
Their silos fill with grain;

Pack up all the camouflage,
Melt every barrel down,
Turn tanks into bicycles
For kids in every town.

Never speak with pride of those
Who gave their lives away,
Nor turn a nostalgic eye
Upon this warring day.

Instead look back to recall
Perspective to your life,
Citing during times of peace
War's devastating strife.

And understand from today
That nations needn't fight,
That men needn't kill nor die
To prove who's wrong or right.

PHYSICAL

"Do you know why we tell you to turn
to the right when we ask you to cough?"
my doctor asks.
"Well, to be honest, I never really thought about it.
I suppose it's because we're exerting
a different pressure when we turn."
My doctor, smiling, turns to me,
snaps on a latex glove, and says,
"Actually, it's so you don't cough all over us.
Turn around and bend over, please."

SIMILE

as a, like a, as a, like a—
to knit with spaghetti
and pepper with mica,
as a, like a, as a, like a—
sail the Serengeti
on a ten-point pica,
as a, like a, as a, like a—
using a simile
as taxing as FICA.

THE CENTURIES CLOSE, ONE AFTER ANOTHER

The centuries close, one after another,
at either end sealed by the methodical
hands of time, the steady and unflinching
hands of advancement: a horizontal gravity
that cannot be slowed let alone stopped.
The seals of centuries, of years, of months
and days can never be opened once closed,
only recalled through the imperfect recollection
that fades into generations of speculation.
Time is neither insidious nor artful;
it has no agenda or ulterior motive.
All that is ever left is the here and now,
the today we can never hope to have again.
Time flows not forwards back backwards.
No one can have tomorrow until tomorrow,
and not even the sun can have yesterday again.
Time will consume each of us outright.
But we are lucky to die, for at least we lived.

THE ADULTERER WAKES

The adulterer wakes and asks the night:

How is it that my flesh burns
  but my sheets stay cool?
How is it that my hair is charred
  but my pillow downy white?
How is it that my heart is ablaze
  but my dog lies twitching, the detector silent?
How is it that my wife lies warm at most
  deep in sleep beside me?
Can she not smell the smoke?
Can she not feel the flames?
Can she in silence unknowingly stoke the fire?
Can she in her faithfulness unwittingly fuel the furnace
  of my conscience?

And the night replies:

Yes! Yes! Yes!
And you can never tell her to ease your burden.
You must forever live in the sleepless conflagration of
  your creation.

Sleep tight.

THE ANSWER TO YOUR QUESTION

You wonder what the hell it's all about,
this thing called life.
You wonder why you even bother,
saying things like, "I'm gonna die anyway."
Then an hour later on the phone with a friend
you gossip like a schoolgirl,
and you catch yourself,
because you're a thinking man,
and you have to sit back and laugh,
because there you are, doing it again,
getting wrapped up in it all, your life,
and you think, if you listen closely,
you may hear in your laughter
the answer to your question.

THE HEART OF THE MATTER

Can we not get to the heart of the matter?
No, for no two can agree upon the matter,
let alone what lies at its core, in its heart.
How, then, may we ever hope to improve?
Well, sadly, improvement is a relative term,
compounded and clouded by the numberless
measurements, definitions and translations
of those with original ideas on the matter.
But are we not all in this thing together?
Oh, yes, the matter comprises us all.
Why, then, can we not find the heart of it?
Because each man believes he is the heart,
when in fact he is merely at the heart.
Do you mean that man's ego is the matter?
For fear of making matters worse, I cannot say.

THE MACHINE

Humming at the frequency of the human heart,
the machine pushes fuel through tubes,
meters it out in precise amounts
designed not to flood the system.
The wheels and cogs of bone and flesh
turn out the energy effortlessly—
a fine-tuned machine indeed.
The operator's job is easy.
In fact, he does nothing at all
while he does it all.

THE POET'S INK

Sadness is the poet's ink,
however varied in shade;
and love, too, will make him think
of words to fill up his page.

THE MEN IN THE MIRROR

During the proudest moments of my life,
when applause or silent gratitude has come over me,
like the pat of my father's hand upon my back,
or even when no other eye but my own
beheld my good deeds,
the best kind of deeds,
I have been happy to behold myself,
glad of who and of what I was.

During the darkest moments of my life,
when mistakes and poor decisions have burned me,
like the sting of my father's strap across my back,
or even when no other eye but my own
beheld my indiscretions,
felt the sting within my conscience,
I have been ashamed to behold myself,
disappointed with who and with what I was.

It is as though, throughout my life,
I have beheld two men with the same face,
each a stranger to the other,
within the eye of my mirror.
My concern is of a third,
which I have yet to see;
and hope is with the first and second
that I will never see
the face of indifference staring back at me.

THE ONE THAT GOT AWAY

BAIT, n. A preparation that renders the hook more palatable.
— Ambrose Bierce

A hitherto unknown child
with flecks upon his cheeks,
with eyes disproved all the while
his well of wonderment leaks,
learns full well the hook of lies
chummed with the tainted bait:
the forbidden fruit under the guise
of what lazy men call their fate.

THE THRUSHES' THREE

The season's a-turning
And leaves are a-burning
In orange and red and yellow:
The coldness imbuing
This vista I'm viewing
With fear of a frosty fellow.

When Winter comes calling
With snowflakes a-falling
Atop these full-wooded highlands,
His crystals replacing
And whiteness erasing
All color as Arctic islands,

A downy ply's hiding
The canvas that's biding
For Spring and Her golden finger,
For maples a-ringing
With thrushes a-singing
In voices three seasons linger.

HARVEST OF SHAME

Harvested from the soil as a weed,
transported and transplanted:
the harvest turned harvester:
fettered to the fields of the white;
stung by the thistle of the white;
enslaved by the greed of the white,
whose careless heads sank deep
into downy pillows of blinding white—
where some still sleep.
Wake up!

TREASURES WITHOUT KEYS

Intention without effort
is the life preserver left on the dock;
desire without purpose
is the shoe on the inside of the sock;
awareness without action
is the kitten stuck high up in the tree;
potential without guidance
is the flower without the bee.

THE REST

The be-all, end-all
we are not.
Our lofty ideals,
our contrived civilization,
our separation from the rest—
the rest of nature—
is pompous at best.
Our struggle is double that of all else,
for we, unlike the rest,
must endure both the natural
and the self-imposed.

THRENODY ON LOSS

Should I stand beyond earth's lamentation,
beyond the sorrow of an anguished heart,
never to know the sting of privation,
then I would be standing a world apart,
beyond the once-loved dawn of each morrow,
and though with you would be cause for sorrow.

STEPPING IN YOUR OWN GUM

Like asking a woman when she's due
and she tells you she's not pregnant.
Like telling the cop who pulled you over
that you only speed after drinking.
Like calling in sick and later that day
running into your boss at the mall.
Like stepping in your own gum.
Sometimes it's better to say nothing at all.

TRACKS

Who left these tracks in this fresh snow?
Some lender for some bill I owe?
Some neighbor with some news to share?
Some peddler with some goods to show?

Two of the three paid for their ware,
Either would call in this cold air
To close a sale or clear a debt,
Though as for that it isn't fair

To rule out all my neighbors yet,
For some want payment, you can bet,
Be it with gossip or a joke,
For stopping by, though I regret.

If number one: sorry, I'm broke;
If number three: see the first bloke;
If number two in want of joke:
See any mirror to invoke.

VILLANELLE FOR LAURIE
(MY SISTER FOUND A GRAY)

Rather to her dismay,
    Atop her auburn head,
My sister found a gray—

Brown-red just yesterday,
    But now appearing dead,
Rather to her dismay.

Should she pluck it away,
    Or color it instead?
My sister found a gray.

"Pluck one and two display,"
    My sister heard it said,
Rather to her dismay;

Dye the strand of decay
    But burn each auburn thread.
My sister found a gray.

Not sure to pluck or pray,
    She climbed back into bed.
Rather to her dismay,
My sister found a gray.

AND TALK ABOUT THE WEATHER

Does it matter what today is like,
whether it's sun or rain?
Will you, the reader, care
or have the least idea—no matter
how eloquently, how exactly
I describe the weather—what today is like?
We all move, some faster than others,
into the shadow of our mortality.
In the end the weather is what it is.
We are powerless to change it.
The weather always wins.

WALKING ON WATER

For any recollection of a wrong
I'd at least one name to shoulder the blame.
I rose as divine as a gospel song:
The weight of the wick; the light of the flame.
When asses like rasps bit into my pride,
Swallowing but mouthfuls of their own teeth,
I pitied their vain efforts while they cried
For death from the dagger beneath my sheath.
For such a self-bedazzled one as I,
Such suffering was difficult to see:
I marked too late the tempest's hungry eye
From which all others had warned me to flee,
And turned to shun it but fell on my seat,
For the sea had frozen about my feet.

WHEN THE PAST KILLS THE FUTURE

You stood like a fog
hiding the sign that points the way home.
No matter where I turned I could not find you.
I could never hope to scale the bastions of your heart.
And though in your hands you held mine,
you could never hope to enter.

YON YEN

The repercussions of gluttony and indolence
beat on the drum of excess: the body submits.
Excess is the tortoise that cuts the ribbon first,
the slow but steady victor laughing at the hare.
What we do or do not do catches up to us all.
We may outrun gluttony, tiptoe past indolence,
but the body remembers—our bones, our organs,
our muscles—and reminds us of our neglect.
Every body aches for moderation, pines for it.

SMUGGLERS' DENIAL

We often refuse the truth,
turning it away,
like a passenger without a ticket.
But it's always there,
a stowaway,
showing up at every station
in our baggage.
We declare nothing,
but we are guilty of smuggling it
wherever we go. The hounds whine.
The inspectors tell us to move along.
Indeed, denied truths are the itches
we can't reach to scratch.
So we pack them away,
stuff them in an extra pair of shoes
we hope we won't have to wear.
And it's only when we're detained
and forced to scrutiny
that we admit they belong to us,
although many still claim they're borrowed.

TEENAGE LOVE

No longer when you touch my leg
do I rise the hungry dog to beg
for the ort you hold above my head.
No, it seems the thrill is dead.
Perhaps not dead but growing old,
the heat between us turning cold:
last year's toys at half price sold
near new ones I have yet to hold.

BREATHLESS IN MAINE

This is Maine in the unpredictable wintertime.
There is no wind today, judging by the larger-than-usual
snowflakes that appear to be suspended from the sky
by invisible gossamers stretching nearly
imperceptibly under the delicate weight of each flake—
dangling midair without the slightest breath of slant.
Oh, like me they fall silently to the highest height.
Breathless in Maine in the unpredictable wintertime.

MARCIA'S FACE WAS OILY

Marcia's face was oily.
She didn't realize it was oily
until I pointed it out,
but it was.

About a week after
I told her,
I saw her again:
her face was dry,
red,
and sore.

Damn!
I'm an idiot!
Marcia liked me.
Marcia liked me a lot.

A FARMER SURVIVED

Too gay grow the flowers
For these solemn hours;
Too blue is the sky today:
Too soon the cream sours,
For time has such powers
To lay sweet life away.

No lilies lie weeping
The harvest that's heaping
Upon his shoulders today:
The son keeps on reaping,
For time ever creeping
Can never be held at bay.

And time, as life's drafter,
May write out the laughter
Loved ones heard yesterday,
But the pickpocket grafter
Can't stop the hereafter,
And together again they may.

MY CAPISTRANO

So soft and low the swallows go,
Their unfettered wings returning—
As I to you in freedom true,
Your absence the cause of yearning.

So with a pace of double haste,
My legs like wings fly home this eve—
No vocal rage, no gilded cage,
Just love and trust and free to leave.

HOLY MACKEREL

The deck shimmered, a sea of mackerels
shining, stinging in the unwelcome moonlight,
moving not by each but by all:
a seamless wave with a common thread
sewn through each of their sequined bodies
sloshing against the boat-walls:
a sea upon a sea, doubly tossed,
my legs buckled, my stomach loosed:
I learned I was not a Christian.

ESPECIALLY BOURBON

My mother tells me with bourbon breath that
love is like a flower, it needs to be watered
and renewed or it will wither and be overrun
by weeds and insects. I nod, half in daydream,
half in contemplation. She pours herself
another drink and asks if I think my second
stepfather will ever return. I tell her I'm not sure.
She lights a cigarette and holds it in her mouth
As she straightens a painting of roses in a vase.
The smoke collects about her head. I rise to leave.
My mother and I share more goodbyes than hellos:
I don't smoke, and I rarely drink, especially bourbon.

I FLY

The memory of his mother's face,
smooth and warm,
like a cup of cocoa on a winter's day,
soothed the burn of loss.

Although he could not remember
suckling at her engorged breasts
like a pup still blind to light,
he imagined such a muted state
and longed to return to that
cocoon of warmth and comfort,
where innocence envelops
an instinct easily turned habit,
a habit stopped only by weaning's
passage into mounting independence—
a loaf difficult to swallow.

But he was forced to fly.
Blown from the nest by the searing wind of grief,
a fluttering fledgling with wings
still bent to the curve of an egg,
he dropped from the sky
with double gravity.

And with his mouth wide open
and his heart a sponge,
his loss came down
like the fist of a judge,
the verdict drowning his dependency
in unwadeable reality:
fend for yourself,

fly or die.

But the memory of his mother's face,
smooth and warm,
like a cup of cocoa on a winter's day,
soothed the burn of loss.

He still soars.

NURSE!

Like stepping off a sidewalk and getting clipped by a car doing a buck ten through a school zone, it's not good. So there you are, writhing in pain in your hospital bed, the morphine auto-injector proving to be inadequate to manage the pain of your busted hip and your fractured femur. And the nurse call button is busted too, unless she's ignoring you because you're a pain in her ass. Besides, she's already been in your room three times in the past fifteen minutes, and she figures that if she has to explain to you again that she can't give you any more drugs, she's going to need some herself. Of course, you know all this but push the damned button anyway. And then it dawns on you that you never did get around to renewing your health insurance policy, and you wonder how the hell you're going to pay for all of this, because this is big time, we're talking fifty grand or more. And you're pissed, I mean furious, and you wonder if you'll lose your house or at least your car, because you know there's no way you can swing this one. You're lazy, a procrastinator to the nth degree, and you know you've really done it this time, screwed yourself royally. And then, to make matters worse—if they could get any worse—a detective comes in and asks you if you saw the car that hit you—the make, the model, the color, the plate number, anything at all. You tell him no and he says that it's unlikely that they'll ever find the person who did this to you, as if it mattered anyway. You put your hands on the sides of your head, grab a couple of handfuls of what little hair you have left, and breathe deeply. Oh, this just sucks. You could count to ten a million times and it still wouldn't change anything, it wouldn't make it all better again, like when your momma kissed your booboos away. Why me, why me, why me?

Oh, poor little man, as helpless as a kitten, reduced to a shadow in the blink of an eye. This is the sort of thing that happens to other people, the stuff you skim past in the daily newspaper. You don't need this crap, and you figure you're going to do something about it. But you're done, and you know it, so you do the only thing you can do right now, but not even that's working. So you just push and push and push and wonder where in hell that goddamned nurse is.

THE GORILLAS' SIDE

The gorilla lumbers to the window,
galumphs his way through his captivity,
ponderously treads with foot and hand on
a world he knows does not belong to him.

He sits, inches from the pane I peer through,
and proceeds to strip a twig with his teeth.
I watch him intently, captivated
by his human-like features and manner.

And then, as though he can sense connection,
he raises his brow and fixes his eyes—
his deep, dark, wise eyes—on my very own.
In an instant afraid yet calm I stare.

I begin to think about humankind,
our existence with other animals,
our global propensity for money,
our growing disregard for each other.

I think of the ruin of rain forests,
the contamination of land and sea,
the depletion of the ozone layer.
I ponder inhumane humanity.

The gorilla's eyes appear sad somehow,
like he feels sorry for what man has done.
My eyes glaze over with regretful tears.
He slowly tilts his head left and then right.

And then, in a surreal occurrence,

he raises an arm and presses his palm
against the glass—to the world between us.
In turn, I place mine cautiously to his.

It is as though he wants to comfort me,
as if he can hear my apologies
and wants to let me know it is alright.
I hang my head in shame and start to weep.

Minutes reveal that we are not alone.
I slowly remove my hand from the glass,
our eyes still fixed deeply on each other's.
He soon lowers his arm and turns his stare.

The gorilla rises and walks away.
I feel empty inside, cold and alone,
like someone has told me of a friend's death.
I turn and leave the viewing area.

Outside I walk around the exhibit,
take deep breaths and try to gain composure.
Now I see the gorillas from afar,
each one captive but seemingly content.

I wonder as I walk away, then turn
to see the gorillas' side of the glass.
At first I am confused by the mirrors,
but then I understand my reflection.

THE MAGIC CONFLUENCE

To become un-animal
he would invent a god,
lest upon his death he find
the wisdom of his dog.

He knew apart from the beast
that he would someday die,
so to numb futility
he turned toward the sky.

To give meaning to his life
he yielded his control,
put his fate in his god's hands
and prayed to save his soul.

He then imposed on others,
so all would pray his way,
the coinage of religion
and edicts of its sway.

But to live without control
was to live as the beast;
for meaning and power both
required lawman and priest.

To be greater than nature,
to become "civilized,"
to distance man from creatures
and all he scrutinized,

He would create his own laws

brimful of punishment,
not of morals and values
but ease of government;

Not in terms of right or wrong
but based on consequence:
his religion and his law:
the magic confluence.

THE MAGIC KITE

I dreamt that I returned to youth
with lively feet as light as air,
had golden locks and rosy cheeks,
and daisies for my mother's hair.

And in my hand I held a kite
upon a never-ending string,
and flew it up and up and up
into the heights where cherubs wing.

And from their clouds so soft and white
they blessed my little kite with care,
and tied to it a silken tail
with bows to soar upon the air.

And up and up and up it flew,
my little kite it flew so far,
right past the moon in outer space,
and hitched itself upon a star.

And holding to that magic string,
the star it carried me away,
past daisy fields of golden wheels
and every place where children play.

And speeding through the Milky Way,
past oceans blue and mountains white,
I blinked my spinning eyes to see
the night turn day and day turn night.

And ever faster than before

the sunlight rose and then it set,
and I outgrew my golden locks
and rosy cheeks of teacher's pet.

And soon the sleepy star it slowed,
and soon my youthful wings had flown,
and so the star it dragged me home
and dropped me in my bed full grown.

And weary from my fancied flight,
I let go the string of my kite,
and watched it as it flew away,
into the darkness of the night.

THE LAST TIME MY FATHER LEFT

The night he packed his suitcase his shoes weighed a little more and his shirts took up a little more space. Everything seemed bigger, exaggerated in the care he took to fold and place each item into the case: the socks not rolled but folded twice and placed next to the underwear, each pair of which had been folded three times (at the crotch and then once on either side) and placed next to the undershirts. The whole case was arranged in such a logical way: shirts next to ties, trousers next to belts. The suitcase itself had been in the attic for the better part of ten years and needed a good dusting off. He would have liked to take it back up to the rafters, put the dust back on it, and relock the attic door on his way down. But that was out of the question. He had to go. He was committed to go. He found his keys, made sure his wallet was in order, kissed me on the forehead, and said good-bye to my mother.

I STRAIN

In this age of distinction, where
we grope in the dark for singularity,
for individuality, for the distinctiveness
of the inseparable, the indivisible *I*,
we search for a pronoun that stands
for either sex equally, shunning
the centuries-old he/his/him and using
instead the plural and thus incorrect *their*.
And while the search continues
for that elusive noun-substitute,
that gender-neutral miracle word which
will at last give each of us equal billing,
a focus on *me* erodes a sense of *us*.

DREADED WASH DAY

The clothes go on and the clothes come off,
the laundry heaps and the laundry heaps,
and I save my quarters throughout the week
   for wash day—
     dreaded wash day!

Whites here, darks there,
keeping jeans from underwear—
a kind of clothing segregation.
Temperature's important, the clothing labels warn:
   hot or cold only—
     I wash all mine in warm.

One load, two loads, three loads and four,
recalling that I've done this a time or two before:
measuring the detergent, pouring in the bleach,
adding the fabric softener and the anti-static sheets.

Washing and drying and folding and pressing,
a never ending cycle of dressing and undressing:
the clothes go on and the clothes come off,
the laundry heaps and the laundry heaps,
and I save my quarters throughout the week
   for wash day—
     dreaded wash day!

MY SWEET STILL LOVES ME

With snow-laden lashes and ruby-red lobes,
A surrey that dashes and warm winter robes,
Sweet and I went riding through the harbor square,
Sending out a tiding to everyone there.
My sweet, she still loves me, after all these years,
And standing proclaimed she to the sound of cheers.
And I, lucky indeed, held the reigns with tears,
For my sweet still loves me, after all these years.

A CONVERSATION WITH MY FATHER

That's tough.
What's tough?
Life.
What's life?
A magazine.
How much does it cost?
A dime.
I only have a nickel.
That's tough.
What's tough?
Life.
What's life?
A magazine.
How much does it cost?
A dime.
I only have a nickel.
That's tough.
What's tough? . . .

FISHING WITH DAD

I remember once when dad and I went fishing,
we didn't have much luck—
we only caught one fish between the both of us.

And even though that old fish took my father's bait,
he let me reel him in, which made my day just great!

Thanks, dad.

SLEEPWALKING AT CHRISTMASTIME

deep in the fog
of this deep forest
I feel for a tree
to anchor to
as I shuffle through
last year's needles
and know there has to be a tree
around here somewhere
and then I find one with my face
and wake from the pain
of my shin meeting a coffee table
and wonder where the hell I am
and whose presents these are
and what they're doing next to a coffee table
in the middle of a forest

FIRST AND LAST

"What's MSG?" my date asks.
"It's an acronym for monosodium glutamate," I answer.
(I can tell this doesn't answer her question,
and I know she wants to ask what an acronym is.)
She nods.
"It makes my lips swell up," she says.
"And your brain, I'll bet," I say under my breath.
"Pardon?"
The waiter comes to take our order.

"I'd like the Hu Nan special, please."
The waiter writes aloud, "H-u N-a-n."
"I don't know, who is Nan?" I ask.
The waiter laughs.

My date stares at me blankly.
To her my wit is witless or too witty.
She is instantly unattractive to me.
I think this will be our last date.

WAKE ME FOR DINNER

Draw those curtains and close that door!
I need to rest my head!
It's only noon and that's too soon
For getting out of bed!

You say that you're concerned, my love,
That I'm getting thinner—
Well, if that be the truth, my dear,
Wake me up for dinner!

MEMORIES OF THE GAME

We had devised plays even the NFL hadn't seen:
Double X, 23 Cross, Devil's Dive;
Lone Back, Statue of Liberty, Flea Flicker Option;
And my personal favorite,
Triple Set, Post Left, Back-breaker . . . on three . . .
"Ready, break!"

The rules were simple:
two completions for a first down;
down and back for a touchdown;
five Mississippi rush with one blitz for every four downs;
the fences and the house were out of bounds;
two hand touch or tackle,
depending on whose yard we were playing in
(some of us had dogs, if you know what I mean).

We played football nearly every day.
We played to play.
We'd take to the backyards of our houses,
each of us wearing *Toughskin* jeans
and grass-stained shirts,
and play for hours.
We were lean (about 85 pounds each)
and mean (we'd spit, burp, fart, and scratch ourselves)
and dirty (none of us bathed—
baths were for sissies and girls).

Yes, indeed, we had it all:
receivers in motion, silent snaps, pump fakes,
on-side kicks, fake punts, and touchdown dances—
just like the pros—even better than the pros!

I usually Q'd. I had a pretty good arm
and could throw a *Nerf* ball in a tight spiral.
Tom Wiseman was my best friend
and my favorite receiver.
He was usually my target,
even if the other guys were wide open—
he was skinny but fast.
We'd play until we couldn't see the ball anymore,
until guys started getting beaned in the face.

None of us went on to play pro ball—
or even college ball, for that matter—
although we all dreamed of it.
But that's okay,
because I don't think my memory of the game
could be any sweeter.

LONGING FOR RECESS

As a child I wondered
how people became what they were:
the streetsweeper,
the mailman,
the cabdriver,
the waitress—
did they, as children,
aspire to become these people?

There was something enviable about it all:
the allure and fascination of the grownup world—
knowing they were out there
doing these fun jobs
while I was stuck in school.

Yes, as a child I wondered
how people became what they were.
Today I know
I wish I still wondered.

METAPHORICALLY SPEAKING: A BASEBALL PLAYER MEETS A GIRL AT CLOSING TIME

"Right off the bat let me say that
I'm no heavy hitter,
and I don't mean to throw you a curve,
I just wanna make sure you don't miss the signal.
Let me take a swing at something . . .
Now, I may be way off base and out in left field—
heck! I may not even be in the same ballpark!—
but at least for now I'm batting a thousand.
I mean, I don't wanna play hardball or anything,
but at this stage of the ball game,
I just wanna make sure I cover all my bases, you know?
I mean, I'd like to get into the swing of things.
I don't wanna strike out.
Look, I just wanna score.
Why don't you step up to the plate?
What do you say, are you in or out?
It's your call."

FAMILY KISSES

I belong to a family in which the women, and even some of the men, insist on kissing me full on the lips upon meeting and departing. I must admit that I'm not particularly fond of this incestuous oral handshake. I didn't appreciate it as a child; I appreciate it less now. Don't get me wrong, I haven't a problem with some small display of affection for loved family members; and I rather enjoy kissing but reserve such oral exchanges for those with whom I have a more intimate relationship. It seems to me that a simple hug would suffice to show the sort of familial connectivity not usually extended to a perfect stranger. My relatives, however, obviously feel otherwise.

How is it, anyway, that these fleshy folds encircling what's probably the second most disgusting orifice of the human body became the flesh with which we show our affection for each other? It seems peculiar to me that we should use this bilabial gate to the oral cavity as a facial handshake. After all, any hole through which we breath, burp, chew meat, and on occasion utter obscenities or spew out other verbal diarrhea—not to mention dribble and bad breath—should be reserved for the mere verbalization of hellos and good-byes. When did kissing family members on their lips become commonplace? I wonder if there's an identifiable moment in time when one man or one woman, be it through curiosity or instinct, pressed his or her lips against a kin's? Whether there is or isn't, this longstanding tradition isn't about to give way to a less intimate acknowledgement of someone's coming or going in my family.

Since it's quite clear to me that kissing in my family is here to stay, I've developed an arsenal of counter-defenses designed to protect myself from unwanted germs, lipstick, spit, and food particles. For those in agreement with my dislike, allow me to share with you some of the tactics I employ to minimize or altogether avoid the proverbial lip-lock with grandma, auntie Jean, or uncle Jim.

First, there's a plethora of well-timed verbal excuses. Some of my favorites include the following:

> "May I borrow your lip balm, this darned cold sore has split open again!"
> "This cold is awful! hope it's not TB. How about a kiss?"
> "Ooh, I wouldn't, this could be herpes."
> "Oh, sorry, I just had tuna with onions and pickled anchovies."
> "I'd love to kiss you but I've got a small cut inside my mouth that's leaking puss."

Okay, I admit that these are not the most tasteful verbal excuses, but I can personally guarantee you that each one will help you dodge the dribble—and that, after all, is the goal.

Sometimes, unfortunately, kissing a relative is simply unavoidable (typically when you're caught off guard or stand in a room as the only relative out of many yet to lay one on grandma at her eightieth birthday party). Whether you are ambushed without an egress or bombarded by a blitzkrieg of busses, there are tactics to ease the trauma of practically being licked by a loved one. It's important here to be tactful and subtle. You can't very well drag your sleeve across your mouth as you exclaim YUCK! You can, however, minimize the trauma of being lipped by a loved one (or worse yet, a not-so-loved one) by receiving the unwanted smack on your cheek. Enter the quarter-turn method.

The quarter-turn method is accomplished by doing just as its name implies: turning your face a quarter turn to either the left or the right just before your lips come in contact with a relative's. I can attest that this is an effective method, for not once in all my years of kiss avoidance has a relative yanked my face back to center to lay one on me. You should be aware, however, that if you're about to kiss a relative who's also about to employ the quarter-turn method, there's an outside chance that you may find yourself lip-locked with the enemy—the complete opposite of what you'd intended. The inadvertent spit-swap happens when you turn a quarter turn to the right and your relative turns a quarter turn to the left, or vice versa. My solution? Keep a good inch or two out of reach until you're certain that you're clear of such a mishap.

You can also try the cough attack, although this one takes a little bit of acting. Simply go into a coughing fit just as you're about to kiss—and I mean buckle right over as if it hurts like hell, and keep it up until you're asked if you're okay. This method can reap long-term benefits because a relative will usually remember that you coughed right in his or her face the last time you had a kiss encounter, which means that they're likely to avoid you, too. To really make this method effective (although usually reserved just for the mushiest and most adamant of kissers) you can completely avoid turning or covering your mouth. And if the relative approaches for a kiss after a cough attack, just go right into another one. Repeat this process until the coast is clear.

Whichever method you choose, I hope that you have success in avoiding the bizarre and rather nauseating custom of kissing relatives smack on their lips. I'm sure that once you've practiced a few of these little gems you'll be well on your way to handshakes and hugs wherever you go. Good luck!

BRUSH STROKES

Each is endowed a canvas clean,
And with each breath we paint a scene
Upon this pure and perfect slate
With lines exact and colors keen.

Every brush stroke records our fate,
All that we do, both small and great:
Every smile and every tear;
Each time we love, each time we hate;

Every second of every year;
Everything that we say and hear.
We paint the portrait till it's whole,
While marking all that we hold dear.

And every stroke exacts a toll.
And every line achieves a goal.
And soon we realize our role:
To be the painter of our soul.

THE OPRAH WINFREY SONG

I don't watch Geraldo
I don't watch Montel
I don't watch any Donahue
Or Sally Jesse Raphael

I don't watch Hardcopy
Or Entertainment Tonight
There's only one show I watch at all
And, man, it's out of sight!

They call her Oprah! Oprah!
They call her Oprah Winfrey
One day she's nice and plump
And the next she is skinny!

They call her Oprah! Oprah!
She's got the very best shows
From out-of-work cross-dressers
To auctioning off her clothes!

They call her Oprah! Oprah!
She's on at nine, eleven and one
Well I'd watch her ten times a day
If they'd play re-runs!

They call her Oprah! Oprah!
And here's one thing I know
Howard Sterns better watch his back
If she goes into radio!

Whoa-whoa-whoa, Oprah! Oprah!

They call her Oprah Winfrey
And here's another thing I know
She's the queen of TV!
Yeah! she's the queen of TV!

WHEN I FOUND THE PLAYBOY

It was the kind of cabinet you just had to open:
about three-feet tall, octagonal, and lipstick red
with golden hinges and a matching latch.
It was ornate from top to bottom.
What was it doing in our home,
out of place amid the rough-pine furniture
and the conservative carpet?
It practically begged to be opened!

It was my father's.
It was strictly off limits.
It was too much for a seven-year-old boy to bear.

I still remember the spanking . . .
and page fifty-three.

UPON READING AN AD FOR PENIS ENLARGEMENT...

I realized that the best way to enlarge your penis is to reduce your ego.

VEGETABLE LOGIC

"He loved onions, not daffodils,"
my grandmum said to me,
explaining why she'd planted
vegetables on granddad's grave.
. . .

"Makes sense to me," I said.
"Makes sense to me."

A RECIPE FOR RESTAURANTS

A barrel, a bushel,
a pinch or a peck,
when it comes to cookin'
I say what the heck!

Just throw it together,
it isn't too tough—
no time to mess with
that measurin' stuff!

Just pour it and stir it
and throw it in the 'wave—
you can read your cookbooks
in the time you'll save!

And when that beeper beeps
to tell you it's done,
that grub'll be hotter
than a smokin' gun!

And after you've taken
your very first bite,
you'll taste why I'll be
eatin' out tonight!

Bon appétit!

JUST DO IT

The sculptor's sculpture's a rock.
No good in his head.
A chisel and a mallet.
The painter's canvas is clean.
No good in his bed.
A brush, paint, and a palette.
The potter's clay is a block.
No good if he's dead.
Some water and a wheel.
The poet's poem's a dream.
No good until said.
Ink and the way I feel.

I LIVE TO SLEEP

They say the average man
Spends one-third of his life in sleep—
This fact I merely state,
For being unlike the average man
I spend one-third awake!

HOITY-TOITY

He is wellborn and well-bred,
Well informed and well-read,
But conspicuously rich.

He's flagrantly well-to-do
And openly referred to
As a snobby sonofabitch!

THE TOILET SEAT

"You never put the seat down!"
My sweet complains to me.
"And what an inconvenience
When I have to take a pee!"

To which I quick reply,
Half mocking my buttercup,
"I never put it down, dear,
Because you never leave it up!"

MY NEUTERED DOG

They say he is fixed—
but his face as a token
says he is broken.

MENSTRUAL PERIOD

Noun: The temperament
of very hot china cups
under cold water.

LOVE AND WINE

Love and wine heighten truth by numbing inhibition,
but too much of either will worsen your condition.
Take both in moderation.

IF YOU'RE GREEDY IT'S TRUE

Financial planning
begins with a piggy bank
and ends with a pig.

A TEASE

Two inhalations,
sharp and short, but only that.
They were not a sneeze.

SKINNY

```
a  a  w  o  a  a
   i     n     l
s  s  t  e  c  l
l  p  h     h
i  l     f  i  e
v  i  a  e  c  l
e  n  b  w  k  b
r  t  a  e  e  o
   e  c  r  n  w
o  r  u
f     s  t  c  h
   o     h  h  i
a  f  r  a  e  p
      i  n  s
b  b  b     t  a
o  o  s  s     n
y  n     h  u  d
   e     e  n
         d  b
         e  o
         r  n
            y
         a
            k
         T  n
         e
         e
```

142

G.A.S.
(GRANDMOTHERS AGAINST SPEEDERS)

Why is it that I'm always getting stuck behind that stereotypical little old lady who drives at half the posted speed limit, the one who bought her car the year that turn signals were optional? You know who I'm talking about. She's the one with the I LOVE BINGO and MY OTHER CAR IS A WALKER bumper stickers. If you're lucky enough to have her behind you, you can recognize her in your rearview as the driver with her hands at ten and two and the periscope coming up from the middle of the seat. But beware! You're not safe just because she's behind you—oh no, you can bet your last nickel that one of her many clones is waiting for you a few blocks down the road.

Sometimes I think she's out to get me. It seems as though she waits for me at major intersections just so she can inch her way into my lane, forcing me to stop and waive her in—"Yeah, yeah, you're welcome—hurry up!" Worse yet is when she waits for me on the other side of a hill and I don't see her until I've topped the hill at I'm-late-for-a-meeting speed. After I've tempted my air bag, dumped coffee in my lap, shouted every obscenity I know and slammed on my brakes before I become intimate with her bumper stickers, I am not a happy commuter.

I think there's a whole army of these snail-loving, prune-juice-drinking, Geritol-taking wit-testers that meets on a regular basis to discuss the finer points of driving someone insane—literally driving someone insane! Grandmothers Against Speeders, better known as GAS, or so I call them, teach members the GAS rules of the road. For example, they teach the GAS turning in traffic method:

Approaching the intersection you plan to turn at, and without exceeding three-fourths of the posted speed limit, gradually begin to slow your vehicle by easing the gas peddle backwards at least three blocks before your desired turn. DO NOT BRAKE AND DO NOT SIGNAL! Braking is a dead giveaway that you are slowing, and signaling is a dead giveaway that you are actually going to turn. If you must signal (police are in the area, etc.), wait until you have come to a stop in the middle of the intersection. An experienced turning pro can actually bring a vehicle to a full stop without applying the brakes at all.

Pay close attention to your lane positioning. For left-hand turns, you must position your vehicle as far to the right as possible to ensure that other drivers will be unable to go around you. Likewise for right-hand turns, position your vehicle to the extreme left of the turning lane. Although other drivers will be tempted to go around, you have effectively taken away that option by obstructing their view of oncoming traffic.

To enhance your turning annoyance, please refer to Chapter 4, Section 2, Sub-section F: Stalling Your Vehicle In An Intersection.

Members of GAS are a unique breed, sporting blue and silver hair, orthopedic shoes, knee-highs and girdles. Doused in asthma-attack-causing perfume a skunk wouldn't wear, they carry out their credo with the fervor of a squirrel before winter. They make unnecessary trips to grocery stores, banks, and beauty parlors during peak traffic hours. They remain undecided at drive-thru windows, wavering between chicken or beef, coffee or tea, french-fries or onion rings. They rummage through their glove boxes for expired coupons to save twenty-five cents on a Big Mac, never realizing that they're at Burger King. They search under their seats for their toll tickets—"It was here just a minute ago. Would you take a personal check?" They wait at green lights until they're certain the lights will eventually change back to red . . . .

And all the while I'm stuck behind them. I'm the one honking my horn, cursing cars equipped with anchors, wishing Scotty would beam me home. I'm the one with high blood pressure and an ulcer a cow couldn't cure. I'm the one thinking of taking stress-management classes and yoga. I'm the one who understands why Thelma and Louise drove off that damned cliff—and I'm quite certain I'd join them if the GAS member in front of me would get the hell out of the way!

But there will be justice, for soon I'll have a calcium deficiency of my own and there'll be no place I need to be and no place I need to go. I will be en route to nowhere in particular, driving so slowly I'd get there faster if I'd put it in park. I will aspire to be the most annoying GAS member of all time, perhaps starting my own chapter. And I will most definitely teach the lesson my coffee-stained crotch is learning on every commute: Those who live life in the fast lane usually get burned.

Beep! Beep!

SUICIDE?

A plummeting man—
as fast as gravity can—
ah! a parachute.

GOLDFISH

The eyes of my child—
innocent, meek, mild—
as blue as any sea,
fixed staring straight at me.

Teardrop after teardrop,
each crystal clear,
each filled with pain,
confusion and fear;

Not a single word spoken
to state an appeal
of this pain so vivid,
this loss so real.

Speak and tell me
why you cry
as I explain
that all will die.

Speak and tell me
what it is you wish,
and tomorrow we'll buy
a new goldfish.

NEVER MIND

Haiku! God bless you.
Excuse me, I didn't sneeze.
Beg your pardon, please?

WHY I DON'T DO CROSSWORD PUZZLES

One across: See six down . . .
Six down: See one across.
I hate crossword puzzles.

WHY PEOPLE COMMIT CRIMES

Sticks and clothes
may scare the crows
but corn will entice them.

"WHERE HAVE YOU BEEN?!"

Enamored is the man
Who excuses friend for wife,
Who rushes from the pub for love—
Or fear of losing his life!

WHY I GOT IN TROUBLE AS A CHILD

Mom, can I . . .
Ask your father.
Dad, can I . . .
Ask your mother.

WHEN THE TRUTH COMES OUT

I have found that champagne
Gets me into trouble—
You say the damndest things
When you drink the bubble!

A BETTER NEIGHBOR

Thinking is hard work,
More so than manual labor,
But if done well and often
You'll make a better neighbor!

OBSTACLES & PERCEPTION

How an obstacle's perceived
Is obstacle enough,
But doubly hard to overcome
If perceived as tough.

THUNDERBIRD DREAMS

Since I wish
that I could fly,
I wonder if birds
wish they could drive?

JESUS DRANK BEER

When one beer leads to two
And a dozen sing "cuckoo!"
With no discipline to leave
A barrel full o' brew—

When I've rolled up my sleeve
To wrestle with the Eve
To wrestle with the morn
And rue the ale I heave—

I swear next time I'm born
I'll do as Good Books warn
And live as though I've sworn
The life of Capricorn!

COFFEE SHOP CADENCE

a hiss, a drip, a drop
time passin' on the clock
gettin' slower, slower, slower

cup number one
cream, no sugar
gettin' lower, lower, lower

the scuff, slide, stomp
on rough pine boards
jingle, change, jingle
in the register drawer

sip, swallow, ahh
at the coffee shop bar

clankin' cups clink
as the coffee drinkers drink
and ask for more

cup number two
same as before
outside comin' in
with the closin' of the door

grind, brew, pour
droppin' drops on the floor
grind, brew, pour
and pour some more

cup number three
I can barely see to see
cream swirlin' down
'neath the steam
drownin' like a frown
in a coffee shop town
I drink and dream

havin' coffee shop fun
shoulda stopped at one
one, one more
call it number four
cream, no sugar
same as before

THE LIFE, AN ACHE, AN ITCH

A gun does not a killer make—
Though a gun was made for killing—
A murderer is one who takes
    the life
Of a target not able or willing.

A heart does not a truelove make—
Though a heart was made for loving—
A paramour may push to slake
    an ache—
But a truelove never comes a-shoving.

A mind does not you learned make—
Though a mind was made for learning—
The feebleminded will forsake
    an itch—
While a wise person scratches the burning.

QUIBBLING TIMES

Politicians quibble,
Circumvent the truth,
Disregard their fathers,
And tighten their nation's noose.

THE WINNER AND THE WHINER

Two fighters:
one speaks of hunger—
not for food but victory;
the other doesn't speak at all—
he just eats.

CANDLE'S CLIME

Flame, flickering in my eye
As if I were a translucent fly
Whose splendid wing you try to burn
But fail as the seasons turn—

Your heart too hot to hold,
Your lips to kiss would scold—

Until winter besets its wrath all 'round
And even the sun falls quicker down,
You will not tempt me to your fire
(Until the frost makes me a liar).

HUMAN SHEEP

Most are inclined by habit,
Through neglect themselves to be,
To hold a consensual view—
Albeit a travesty.

THE CIRCLE OF LIFE

Of calamity I have sung
With words of sullen sake—
Given lift to many a-one
Whose love does no more wake—
Whose cherished kiss no longer fills
Departure nor return—
Whose memory forever stills
The heart that once did burn.

For mothers new I have rejoiced
With words of fitting glee—
And heard the cry that is first voiced
A wordless newborn plea—
A shrill reminder that the grief
So oft within the soul—
Is but the wind that turns the leaf
And makes the circle whole.

I LEARN MORE ON SUNDAY MORNINGS

I learn more on Sunday mornings than I do all week.

Lying long in my bed,
stubborn to the sun and the uncut grass,
Max, my German shepherd,
licks my hand,
flops on the bed,
sighs from the effort it took to join me.
His sigh is my sigh,
here in slow time
on Sunday morning.

DISSOLVE

Handsome man,
soft eyes and hands—

patience, willpower—
do what you can—

breast cupped
in the palm of his hand . . .

and you.

AT LAST MY FATHER IS WISE

I remember what you said,
that someday you'd be wise
in my eyes.
I wore a know-it-all smirk
and seriously doubted your sanity.

Revelations later,
I hear it said:
"A prophet is without honor
in his own land."

Dad, I know now that it's true.

LOVE'S CORNERSTONE

Empty hearts cannot refrain
From misery and sorrow—
Lest some soul loves them
Ensures their pain tomorrow.

Such hearts love not themselves
And thus avert attention—
'Tis the nature of the man
Who rues his own dimension.

To truly love another
One must love himself—
For self-love is the cornerstone
Of love itself.

DÉJÀ VU

```
                    My
            today        days
             of           and
           sameness      nights
            the          revolving
           hours         spinning
          indifferent      me
             in          dizzy
             me          with
              drowning  boredom
                    and
```

IN PRAISE OF NATURAL DISASTERS

Each day the world gets smaller,
like it's a balloon with a small leak
hurtling through space,
making that obnoxious farting sound
as it spins out of control,
its axis broken and
unmendable,
like its hell bent on being the center of the universe—
in spite of Copernicus
and his little discovery.

The shorelines shrink.
Masses swell inward and outward,
imploding and exploding
upon each other,
still trying to claim their stake,
to rule their way,
to own the wind.
(You'd think we'd know better by now.)

Resources grow scarce,
controlled and contracted,
bought and sold in a dizzying cycle.
Millions go hungry.
The well-fed want more,
waste more,
give less.

And then a beautiful thing—
a typhoon,
an earthquake or a landslide,

a flood or a hurricane,
a volcanic eruption or a tornado—
makes space,
claims the lives of thousands.
The living mourn for a moment—
then, like lions distracted from the kill,
clamber for a piece of meat
and a drink
to wash it down.

ALL I AM IS ALL I KNOW

All I am is all I know
And that's all I'll ever be:
Understanding limited
To my vocabulary.

I know what I have words for—
Not anything more than this—
And that alone proves to me
That ignorance isn't bliss.

(To broaden your horizons,
To enrich your fallow mind,
Go sow the seed of language
And reap knowledge from its vine.)

BECAUSE I LIVED

Non omnis moriar.

The sand will outlast my intentions.
The sea will survive my memory.
The sky will not remember my voice
or my thoughts or my dreams or my desires.
The sun will forget it ever shone upon me.
And still I live for today and hope for tomorrow—
it is all I can do—
all I was ever meant to do.

Yes, the world will go on:
The sand and the sea, the sky and the sun,
the air that carries the music of my life
will endure my flesh and my bones.
But all will be forever changed
because I lived.

Because I lived
and built sandcastles and swam in the sea;
because I cried and hoped and prayed;
because I breathed the world will be changed
and it will not remember how.
But I will tell you how:
It is because I lived.
Because I lived.

TWO LITTLE THINGS

No matter how clever our machines
Or how well we save our golden beans;
No matter how high we learn to fly
Or build our buildings into the sky;
No matter how fast we learn to go
Or how many worlds we come to know;
No matter how large our brains expand
Or how exceedingly tall we stand—

Civilization would hang from a rope
Without two little things called faith and hope.

THANK YOU

The war in Kosovo,
the shootings in Littleton,
the local girl whose murder
has yet to be solved,
the philandering politician,
the mercury in the fish—
how easy to become hopeless
in our hapless age.
I could complain,
about this or about that,
but perspective lulls me,
rescues me from melancholy
with thoughts of you.
My whole world turns in your eyes.
How well I have it!

BRAINKEEPING

Give me a vacuum for my brain
to suck up all this clutter—
all this useless, senseless crap
muddying my mind.
Give me a towel to dry up
half-remembered things.
Give me a mop to soak up the stains
left by TV sitcoms—
wring out the commercials
and the weather reports.
Give me a sponge to wipe away
passing conversations,
bits of songs, background noises.
Bleach my conscience.
Give me a clean brain
and let me start over again.

MEMORY'S COMPLEXION

I found myself in the eyes of a wrinkled stranger
languishing in memory's smooth complexion.
What stint of life, I thought,
could spare me the reflection?
What food or drug or exercise
could save me from the form?
This I thought until the stranger moved
the mirror in his eye.
And in a moment I cherished youth,
marked my blessings and lived for the day—
feeling the smooth complexion
of a wrinkled stranger's yesterday.

LITTLE BOY, WITH KNAPSACK TIED

Little boy, with knapsack tied,
A day's change of clothes inside,
Lump in throat, but no tears cried—
Son, you have your father's pride.

Tell me, boy, where will you go,
And who'll reap the pain you'll sow?
Who'll give you another try;
Who'll love you as much as I?

Oh, son, I have filled your shoes,
I have paid my childhood dues
And endured those youthful woes—
Battled those parental foes.

I once knew it all, I thought;
Rebelled against what was taught.
But, with the passage of time,
Realized that I was blind.

And, with passage of the same,
How smart my parents became.
Someday you'll also take heed
To that which you've disagreed.

But, for now, these words I say:
With the passing of these days,
Youth is short and wears away—
So, while you can, go and play.

Time to be a man shall come,
Comes to every father's son,
Little boy, with knapsack tied,
A day's change of clothes inside.

THE SUN ALSO RISES, BUT WHY?

Ah! to postulate
after four glasses of wine
is much fun indeed.
My normal inability
to make sense
of life's futility
is impaired to the good sense
of those who don't think at all—
but doubly difficult to cope with
in the morning.

SLICE OF LIFE

Every man has a share,
A slice he cannot count;
No ledger to reflect
What's left in his account.

For every bit of joy
There's a bit of pain;
For every birth, a death;
For every loss, a gain.

And he is richest who,
At the end of his clock,
Finds his way to Heaven
And leaves behind his stock.

OUR LOVE, OUR LOVE

The water doesn't know
When the glass is full;
The glass if it's wet or dry—

And the wind doesn't blow
Knowing push or pull;
The kite if it's in the sky.

BLISS?

In the confines of a shallow mind
There is no diligence;
No will to reason nor understand,
Not even ignorance.

So, to the person who coined the phrase,
I'd like to say just this:
Of all the things I have found,
Ignorance is furthest from bliss.

I GROW MORE LIKE MYSELF

Climbing with no foothold
Into the balance of my life,
To find answers or contentment,
The harmony in strife,
I am reaching ever higher
In age and in understanding,
And grow more like myself
With each day I am withstanding.

MY EDEN'S AURA

Cool in my garden's
dew in the morning
with sassafras sweet
and berries adorning
the aura of my Eden,
I take to a seat
of granite and vine
with mossy legs
of time's design
half-sunken on one side
into a hungry soil.

I am full-lunged,
ravenous and gnawing
on Nature's bones.
I am more than alive,
and I suck the marrow
from this feast
of intoxicating splendor
until it consumes me
wholly in its rapture
and I long to be
more than human.

But it has me and I not it,
I cannot hold its motion.
It has no permanence
but that which moves my soul
and that which is its own
perpetual change.
I am jealous in reverence,

humbled by its subtle conceit,
for it knows its power
and I my lack
with every breath it takes.

I am utterly reduced
by its perfect complex
to the atoms that I am.
My duties fade to trivial
and all I am seems useless.
Yet somehow I am greater,
richer for my visit
to my garden cool,
invigorated and refreshed,
more awake and alive
and ready for the day.

Oh, but if duty never called—
if the hands never reached the mark
when another owns my time—
I swear that I could sit and sit
here my whole life through.
And perhaps ages away
some traveler would find me,
a pile of satisfied bones,
and have the sensibility
to think my plight romantic
and be inclined to join me.

But no traveler will find me here,
defying or succumbing.
No, I have mouths to feed
and debts to pay

and people who expect.
I have human obligations.
But, oh, to sit in my garden's
dew in the morning
with sassafras sweet
and berries adorning
the aura of my Eden . . .

EVERY DAY AT FIVE

The news depresses—
My hope regresses—
Your love refreshes—
In that order—
Every day at five.

X

He had the brawn,
He had the brains,
Yet cursed his purse
In sharp disdain,

For he had all this—
Even the skill—
But all was naught,
For he lacked the will.

THREE MORTAL VERSIONS

1. The Optimist

Out of a mother's womb
And into mortality:
Subject to an end from the start.

Nothing beyond the tomb
Exists of humanity—
Save the love in a human heart.

2. The Pessimist

Out of a mother's womb
And into mortality:
Subject to an end from the start.

Toward impending doom
With doubtful morality—
The poison of the human heart.

3. The Realist

Out of a mother's womb
And into mortality:
Subject to an end from the start.

The struggle we assume
Amid sensed futility—
The nature of the human heart.

BIBLE AND BIG BANG
(a parody of Robert Frost's *Fire and Ice*)

Some say the world's from the Bible;
Some, the Big Bang.
From what I know about libel
I hold with preliterate tribals.
But if I died and Heaven rang,
I think I know enough of Hell
To say that all creation sprang
From God's own well—
The whole shebang!

IN-LAWS

Our unwanted guests have gone.

We sit on the porch,
glaring at each other,
speechless in our separate thoughts:

I want to write,
you want to read,
we can bring ourselves to do neither.

We sit,
domestically shell-shocked,
secretly hoping they'll never return—

but not admitting to each other
such an inhospitable thought.

AN EPIC IN A SENTENCE

When unto Heaven my soul is taken
Upon the wings of dutiful seraphs;
When worldly wisdom has been forsaken
And God dispatches angels as sheriffs;
When not one man has any need at all
To prove his strength nor his wit to any;
When not a single woeful tear shall fall
And worth isn't measured by the penny;
When hearts are true and life isn't measured
Against the actions of a time gone by;
When all spirits are equally treasured
And the river of bias has gone dry;
    Once I haven't a need for repentance
    I shall write an epic in a sentence.

HEADS OR TAILS?

Success or failure? That depends.
Nature has given man two ends:
One end to sit and one to gain;
One holds air; the other, a brain.
And he who has reason to toast
Likely uses the right end most.

Whether man succeeds or fails
Often depends on heads or tails.

FALLING ASLEEP ON MY SOFA
ON A SATURDAY AFTERNOON

The day drags by,
Noiseless and ordinary;
My mouth opens wide,
Says nothing extraordinary.

My eyes water over
In spite of mortality;
Tomorrow may not come
At all or with charity.

QUEST EONS

Am I time's master or it mine?
Wizard of words or slave to rhyme?
Does life have me or I have life?
Does solace make a woman my wife?
Am I a pawn on God's chessboard?
Or is God moved by his own lord?
If asking such as this is dumb,
Please, brain, let this poem be done!

. . .

Thank you.

PLUS SIGN

As restless as a Chihuahua on speed,
I paced the room:
The box said three minutes,
but you'd been in the bathroom for an hour.
I banged on the door
with the persistency of
a mother-in-law who knows you're home—
"Are you okay in there?"
"Just a second," you kept saying.
"What's taking so long?"

Finally, you emerged,
stood there, said nothing.
I tried to read your face,
but it was closed like stone.

"Well?"

You didn't utter a word.
Instead, you raised your hand,
the bathroom light illuminating
your silhouette in half-light,
and slowly turned
your open palm toward my face.

Squinting for the answer,
I asked,
"What does it say?"

Our eyes met,
the corners of your mouth turned up
ever so slightly,
and you whispered,
"It says 'Daddy.'"

RUBBLE TROUBLE

As a child, footloose and fancy-free,
There was nothing at all that worried me:
My face sported a grin and a bubble,
And I often went looking for trouble—
I had no need whatsoever to fret,
I'd survive any punishment I'd get.

I'm now a grown-up child,
And there are many things that worry me:
My face now wears a scowl and some stubble,
As I try to find my way through this rubble
Of endless toil and rivers of sweat,
Hoping there's light at the end of debt.

THE MARROW OF MIRTH

Laughing at yourself
until tears roll down your face
is a great healer.

PRINCESSES AND PEAS

There is an ecstasy
No temperance can ward—
No might or will of man
Will the rapture afford—

Higher than we is this—
Though asses disagree—
But fools always believe
The princess is a pea.

STILLBIRTH

My husband wakes early,
runs to the bathroom and vomits.
Later he develops cravings
for pickles and chocolate ice cream,
green olives with mustard and bacon bits.
This goes on for some time.
Over months his belly begins to swell.
He starts to diet but it's no use,
he just gets bigger and bigger.
Now he's moody and complains of cramps,
hasn't had a bowel movement in a week
but pees every five seconds.
We decide that something's wrong.

At the doctor's he complains to me
that his body aches and that his feet are swollen.
He paces the reception room,
both hands pressed into his lower back.
Finally we're in.
The doctor half-listens,
doesn't make eye contact.
After vital signs, a little probing and a urine sample,
the doctor's back with the diagnosis:
"Well, it looks like you're pregnant,"
he says nonchalantly.

My husband is speechless.
Agape, he turns to me.
My eyes turn to slits and my lips
to a vindictive smile.
"B-b-but how?" he bumbles.

I raise my eyebrows and shrug,
my shoulders rising in implication.
He turns to the doctor.
"Let's take a listen to that belly of yours,"
the doctor says as he motions my husband to a table.
"How can I be pregnant? I'm a man!"
he exclaims to the doctor.
"Stranger things have happened.
Stranger things have happened."

The doctor presses his cold stethoscope
to my husband's drum
and listens for a beat.
Goosebumps rise on *my* arms
and I shudder from intoxication.
"How will it fit through my urethra?
How will you get it out of my penis?"
My husband asks fearfully.
The doctor just sits in concentration.
"I guess you'll have to have a c-section,"
I offer matter-of-factly.
My husband jerks his head around,
his bottom lip trembling,
his eyes as big as full dilation.
I shrug as before.
And then, with impeccable timing,
"It sounds like twins," the doctor says.
My husband passes out.

I open my eyes to find my husband's hand
resting on my flabby, stretch-marked stomach.
I lift it off and roll away to my side,
pushing the blankets into a wall between us.

He moans in his slumber.
I get up, stare at the empty crib,
and doubt I will try again.

PERFECT CHOICE

God's last insult to his own creation,
The permanence of death's a fixed refrain
Between the anger and lamentation
That tempts the soul and crucifies the brain
Of he who remains to question his faith
And suffer the indignation of death,
While his eyes see nothing more than a wraith
And so quickly leave him gasping for breath.
But if from perfectness, why the trial,
If in His image we are created?
Why the temptation of the devil's smile?
Perhaps God's love has been overstated?

You ask what we have from a perfect Lord
That could prove we are loved and not abhorred?
Listen closely to this belief I tell,
Shared with me once but remembered so well:
He is our Father, more than paternal,
For he gives not life but life eternal.
He does not need to prove to lowly us
The exact measure of his perfect love.
Given to bear more than we think we can,
We need to prove to turn boy into man,
For God speaks to each with a varied voice,
But bestows upon all a perfect choice.

THE SNAIL'S ANSWER
(inspired by Wislawa Szymborska's poem *Conversation with a Stone*)

I came across a snail
withdrawn into its shell.
I tapped on its spiral
and asked if I could come inside.

"Why do you want to come in here?" it asked.
"It's dark and there's no room."

"I want to see how you live," I said,
"how you beat time in your carefree way;
how you get everything done
and sleep most of the day."

"You can't come in.
There's no place for you to sit,"
said the snail.

"Please, just for a minute," I said.
"Share your secrets with me.
Just one secret and then I'll go."

"I'm sorry," said the snail,
"but you can't come in.
There isn't even room for you to stand.
Besides, I have no secrets to share.
There is no time for secrets."

"But I won't stay long," I said.
"I have commitments.

Please, teach me your patience;
your economy of time.
It won't take long, I swear."
"Patience is indefinite," said the snail.

I tapped on the snail's spiraled shell.
I tapped again and again.

There was no answer.

PROUD AS ONE

Flag, you are not flung;
Today the wind's asleep—
If, in every foreign tongue,
This way could only keep—
Proud we should be, as one—
Not each.

VINEGAR AND WINE
(a country song)

You tried to be a free man too soon
Growing up with a silver spoon
But momma didn't know
And daddy didn't show
Youth died like the morn with noon

You say you wanna be a man
You wanna understand
What it's like to live your life
You don't wanna be alone
You wanna make a home
You wanna make a woman your wife

CHORUS:

Take some advice, take five for a while
Don't give up, 'cause that's not your style
Just slow down so that you can speed up
When your heart's ready and your mind's tough
Because good things come to those who wait
It's patience that makes a good man great
Remember grapes plucked soon from the vine
Make good vinegar but lousy wine

You tried to win every single race
In an unrealistic pace
But the distance went on
And your wind was soon gone
And you finished in last place

You say you have no time to play
You have to work today
And you shoot your kids a wink
So they grow in the dark
And as adults depart
In retrospect a blink

(Repeat Chorus)

THE PERSUASION OF SANCTIMONY

Bewildered, as a man can be,
I fight to keep my sanity
As masters of hypocrisy
Scream their self-righteous words at me.

Oh, there appears to be a breach!
Shouldn't they practice what they preach?
It seems the people they beseech
Shouldn't listen to what they teach.

Want spiritualization?
Provide some rejuvenation
By keeping your big donation
For your own administration.

THE SHAPE OF LOVE

Because love is round
I have found
I can never arrive at its station—

As distant as the horizon's lair
And distant still once there
At what was just its location.

Because love is square
It isn't fair
That all sides must be equal—

Though that being said
I prove in short leg
That solitude's the sequel.

LOVE IS . . .

Finding someone whose
definition
is the same as yours.

MIDNIGHT STROLLS ON BACK-COUNTRY ROADS AND CARS THAT COME OUT OF NOWHERE

(Lost in stars . . .)

Honk!

(I exhaled the gasp now relief
hot against the air;
embalmed its mist—
my life—
on my face
until the intoxication
dissolved at my door.)

Watch where you're going!

POSTCARDS FROM HELL

Should angels be
upon my death;
if I find God
in my last breath;
if Heaven is
and Hell is too
and Jesus reaches
out to you
but extends
no hand to me,
let him know
I loved you so
but hated
hypocrisy.
And if he asks
you to explain,
simply say
I was profane—
not because
I was a pigeon,
but that I had
no religion.

Think of me
in my flames and locks
as you fly
to your mailbox.
Since we're parted
I would do well
to write and send
postcards from Hell—

I hope the Devil
can digress
to share with me
your new address.

MY FRIENDS

Friends abound gather 'round
And offer their advice—
They expound and astound,
Which I suppose is nice—

But if the truth be told,
All secrets off the shelf,
I love friends more than gold,
But learn more by myself.

CAFFEINE AND CONSCIENCE

I'm coaxed to sleep
        by persistent drops
of rain outside my window,
        off to dream about
things I won't recall
        in the morning when
I eat my toast
        and sip the coffee
I shouldn't drink
        because it's bad for me
and keeps me up
        if I drink it just
before I go to bed
        and think about sleeping.
Unless it's raining
        and the cadence calms
my racing mind
        and I'm able to focus
just on raindrops
        trickling out a lullaby
as my sweet mother did
        before I was too big
to be tucked in,
        before I even liked coffee
or needed to stay awake
        for anything anyway,
I'll be up all night.

FUMBLING WITH CHANGE: FOOTPRINTS ON THE WALL

We sneaked out of your bedroom—
footprints on the wall—
at midnight when we were fourteen
to meet two pretty girls
with footprints all their own.

Yes, indeed, we were cool—
Freezing, in fact, outside the *Seven Eleven* store.
Our parents let us do this—
except for school nights, of course—
we were men!—
complete with an armpit hair each.

We flipped a coin to see
who would carry the condom—
the same condom we'd had
since the third grade—
the same condom we had
until the eighth grade—
you washed it in your jeans,
remember?
I could have killed you!
Our "insurance policy"—
or so we called it
(too much TV, I guess)—
washed and dried and gone.
I knew I should have kept it.

Oh, well, the pharmacy was fun—
watching you buy "rubbers"

or "prophylactics"
as the pharmacist said
when he corrected you
in front of the women waiting in line
while you fumbled with change.
I thought your cheeks would explode!
I'd never seen anyone that red before.

Man, we sure had some good times.
Even the bad times seem good now.
Like after our rendezvous
with those girls at *Seven Eleven*—
I never would have guessed
your dad could fit in your bedroom closet.
He's a scary man in the dark!

It seems another world
and a million years ago:
I'm in New Hampshire now;
you're still in Colorado;
I sell insurance;
you're a bartender.
I'm not sure who's doing better.
I suppose it doesn't matter.

Oh, well, years and miles removed,
here's a toast to innocence,
and to footprints on the wall.

NUTCRACKER

My sister used to crack nuts with her teeth—
not peanuts, anybody can do that—
I'm talking about real nuts—
Brazils and hazelnuts.
"We don't have dental insurance, you know?"
my father would warn,
some sort of implied consequence,
instead of telling her to use the nutcracker.
But she was such a tomboy—
in one ear and out the other.

She called me yesterday,
excited about her newest boyfriend—
some friend of a friend of a friend.
Out with the old and in with the new.
The flavor of the month.
"That's great. Just be careful." I warned,
some sort of here-we-go-again reply,
instead of telling her to use the nutcracker.
But that's my sister—you gotta love her—
twenty years older
and still cracking nuts with her teeth.

A DECORATED SOLDIER

She's thirty-nine,
has been for years,
spends a fortune on
wrinkle cream and hair color,
combats the big four-o
with chemical warfare.

But, much to her dismay,
the truth-illuminating sun,
at just the right angle,
strips her naked,
exposes every
crack in the porcelain.

The crow's-feet stubborn
to the oncoming veil
scratch and claw a deeper
foothold into her expression,
with every squint enhancing
the latent face of age.

With the enemy fortified,
frustration gaining way
for acceptance amid
her struggle to assume
the irretrievable complexion
of porcelain fresh from the kiln,

she relinquishes her weapons,
their importance waning
in the maturity of perspective,

and surrenders to the good sense
that she will always be
a beautiful soldier.

ON THE HORIZON

The sun doesn't rise,
Nor does it set—
The world turns on its axis—

And daylight's the prize
For nighttime's debt—
As sure as death and taxes.

BE THE AUTHOR OF YOUR LIFE

My life, it seems, a book of days
Written in perfect paraphrase
On the parchment of my mind.

It is as though the pages turned,
The chapters closed, the lessons learned—
Moments I have left behind.

Each breath a sentence in my book,
My eyes full blind to cast a look
Upon what tomorrow brings—

As though each page unturned ahead
Lies tightly sealed and unread
Until each new morning sings—

And I with every pulse and whim
Write without a pseudonym
Today to shape tomorrow.

Dog-eared and yellowed lies my prime;
No man a way to lend me time—
Nor I the means to borrow.

So, with chapters ever fewer,
The reeling days my line and lure,
I write in lasting glory—

For when my book reaches its end
It will be too late to amend
The pages of my story.

So to myself is this advice:
Whether in harmony or strife—
Be the author of your life!

Be the author of your life!

CLOSING VOYAGE

Let the compass point rightly
To the port I wish to get;
Let all skies at night be red
Until the anchor is set;
Let the fabric catch the wind
And no latitude impede;
Let the keel cleave the water
And the tempest's wrath recede!

Let all these and let one more,
Gracious keeper of the dome:
Let my love wait by the shore,
For her sailor's coming home!
Her sailor is coming home!

LIVE, LIVE, LIVE, LIVE

Be my summers bereft
With just thirty left,
I live as though this is my last,
For too many learn late
That days dissipate
And the present becomes the past.

And for autumns the same,
If thirty remain,
May I relish every hour,
Unlike those who assume
The fields always bloom
And that frost won't kill the flower.

And If winter appears
For thirty more years
To numb me with shivering cold,
I hope to remember
Each deep December
That not every dear friend grows old.

And if blossoming springs
Crown flowers like kings
For thirty more seasons or one,
May I take what they give
And live, live, live, live
Like tomorrow may never come!

THE BLADE OF BIAS

Dull the mind and thick
Where a bias will grow—
Sharp the blade and quick,
And the bandage too slow.

Sharp the mind and quick
With no bias seeded—
Dull the blade and slow,
And no bandage needed.

MY DOG DOES NOT BLUSH

My dog does not blush
when he has gas.
In fact, he never blushes.
Not once has he apologized
for digging in the yard,
for barking at the mailman,
or for chasing the cat.
He has never complained about his life
or turned to the sky for answers or forgiveness.
He has never obsessed over his weight
or pored over beauty magazines
for exercises to trim his thighs.
He does not fuss with his hair,
nor does he care what others think of his hair.
He knows no shame, remorse or guilt.
In short, my dog is not human.

INSTANT KARMA
(a true story)

I see something moving out of the corner of my eye.
I turn to see a man on a bicycle
pedaling down a gravel path on the other side of the road.

He rides by, as if in slow motion,
and shoots me a rude stare that asks,
"What in hell are you doing parked there?"

He extends his middle finger to me.

Just then his bike's front wheel slams into a tree stump.
He goes airborne, still staring at me,
then crashes in a heap to the ground,
a pile of metal and flesh.

I blink once, casually face forward, pull the car into drive,
and slowly pull away.

CONVERSATION CLOSED

you speak of dogma
        i don't abide
the words you use
        to my views chide
and though i take
        your eyes in stride
i bite my tongue
        and swallow my pride
and wince at every
        word of snide
not because
        your words deride
or make a mockery
        as they divide
but rather because
        i realize
you're too stubborn
        to compromise

COMET

Comet, with your tail streaming
    across the Milky Way,
Heavenly sister of Orion
    over a sky in May,
This pinnacle's a pittance
    of what a man would need
To hold your splendor in his hands
    and sow your celestial seed;
Just a place where the ground
    lifts otiosely toward
That state of blissful oblivion
    found only heavenward.

Heedless of this mass
    and the dilemmas of the day,
Heedless of this time and place,
    the people's apprehensive sway,
I hold you mirrored in my mind
    in the purest state
And humbly give my insignificance
    to drown in your spate;
I give my realization,
    above man and earth,
That I know in comparison to yours
    what my life is worth.

THUNDER'S SONNET

He is an ogre of the moonless night,
Floating in darkness over those he spies,
Gloating in starkness with attentive eyes
For children dreaming of high-flying kites
With their tails streaming in the highest heights.
Silently he creeps, with dark wings he flies,
Through the night he peeps, his patience soon dies.
He's veiled and vulgar with an appetite.

From within the clouds he makes his choice,
Collects a deep breath, rears his ugly head,
Pulls away the shroud, lets lightning rejoice.
Finally, like death, with deafening tread,
Thunder howls aloud with a startling voice,
And the babes know death sleeps under their beds.

A WOMAN'S WORK

A man's work is from sun to sun,
but a woman's work is never done.

She lay down,
still in her work clothes,
beaten by the day:

her knees pulled to her chest,
the blanket to her chin,
a thirty-nine-year-old embryo—
      much to her mother's chagrin.

AND YOU THOUGHT TRIGONOMETRY WAS HARD

Bless the monk who wakes with an erection.
Saint or sinner?
There's no perfection;
No distinction,
despite genuflection.
The body laughs at celibacy
when the mind's asleep—
even in a monastery.

A TALE TWICE TOLD

A tale twice told
To the teller becomes truth—
As the haggard woman
To the drinker
Slowly returns to youth.

Both are self-sought fantasies
That blur the inner eye—
But in the morn
When sobriety comes
Both remain a lie.

FREE YOUR MIND

You should right your wrong.
Within a guilty conscience
no man can be free.

WE SHOULD HAVE BEEN A-GIVING

I gave nothing when I could—
Not one pittance, not one iota.
I gave to me, as I thought I should,
To satisfy my greedy quota.
Many about me did the same,
Their purses were frugal and tight—
We ate caviar and sipped champagne
For many a-day and night.

And then it happened—we lost it all,
And for help from others we pleaded—
But no one had any means at all
To provide the help we needed.
Now we know that when we had
We should have been a-giving,
For now our lives are worse than bad
And barely worth a-living!

UNDERSTANDING

We would get along
if only we could listen
as well as we hear.

DIGITAL MAN

He drives the newest cars
with the most advanced features
and technological breakthroughs;
lives in a house that's wired
from foundation to roof
with satellite dishes and security systems;
has DVD's, CD's, lasers and more;
owns the fastest computers,
mobile phones, pagers and toys;
has facts and figures at his fingers;
in short, he owns the best of every
gadget and gizmo made.

I've yet to meet a man who knows less than he.

SO LIKE CHILDREN ARE THE AGED

So like children are the aged,
Though in different circumstances,
For both rely on faith and friends,
But children have second chances.

SAYDOBE

Saying you are intelligent because you have a degree is like saying you are well-read because you have a library card.

Saying you are a good person because you believe in God is like saying you are a good person because you believe in noodles.

Saying you are a good friend because you buy expensive gifts is like saying you are a good parent because you never beat your child.

Saying you are trustworthy because you have never stolen is like saying you are innocent because no one has blamed you.

Saying you are this or that doesn't make it so. It isn't until you do that you can be. And then you are.

Say. Do. Be.

REVERSAL REHEARSAL

You cannot hold your breath
And make things go away—
Children are tomorrow
The parents of today.

The lessons taught at home
Can free youth when they're old—
Or render them useless
If that's what they've been told.

You'll find in your children
The likeness of your heart—
Since soon they'll care for you,
Are they up for the part?

THE HANDS GO ROUND

The hands go round
And the sun comes down
And the moon chases it;

The birds will sound
When morning's crowned
And light embraces it;

The world is round
And we're upside down
But we're not falling off;

The masses sound
When their kings are crowned
But the sun sets and scoffs;

For days are round
And curtains come down
And everything's the same;

For birds may sound
And kings may be crowned
But the moon's quest is vain.

A SELFISH MOTHER

Fast as still,
She changes details
as subtly as Her cohort Time.

She moves,
a thread through an eye,
pulling the stitches crumbling tight
until the curtain is drawn—
and I hate Her with naked arms
until She returns the beauty She loaned me.

Ah! spring!
and love again.

WOODCHUCK

Tell me, little woodchuck sniffing the wind,
what is the scent that is your fondest?
I am watching you so intently,
I am sure you can feel the weight of my stare.

IF ONLY EARTH HAD A SPIN CYCLE

The colors go 'round
so fast, so close, they are one
at the *Laundromat*.

SHARING YOUR BLINDNESS

Rest you well,
for soon tomorrow comes
as light of day
to melt the dark of night away:

The sun will shine,
the moon will fade,
the stars will all but be displayed,
and then I will wish,
as you do,
upon something there that can't be seen.

AT THE EDGE OF INNOCENCE

In the solace of sleepless moonscapes;
In slow time at my mind's window;
At the edge of remembering innocence;
While my world sleeps deep in ignorance;
As faces fade with songs I sang,
Games I played, hearts I won and lost—
I wish the carousel intrigued me as it used to.

POLITICS AND RELIGION

The only time I open my mouth is to switch feet.

THE RULES

I'll use good for well
and me for I
and no one can tell me why
I disobey the rules.

I'll use can for may
and curse all day
and not hear a thing you say
about the rules.

I'll use are for am
and that for which
and scratch at this awful itch
you call the rules.

I'll use got for have
and who for whom
and I say it ain't too soon
to dump the rules!

I say damn the rules!

HOLLOW WORDS

Hollow words of no intent—
When professed a pledge—
Can inflict greater damage
Than a razor's edge.

HISTORY

History doesn't dictate destiny.
It's important to know from where you came,
but only to measure how far you've come—
or haven't.

A JUMP FROM REASON

The whole world stopped when I jumped from reason
in the summer of '79.

The landing of the iron stairs seemed a mile from the tar,
a mile from freedom from the taunts of my playmates.
I sat on the rusted slats, wiggling my way to the edge,
trying not to look like the chicken they were calling me.

I was nearly ten and new to the States from England.
Kids new me as the boy who "talked weird."

"Jump!" they shouted, frustrated from their own clucking.
I inched closer, my sweaty palms signaling the dilemma,
feeling the momentum of the situation mounting
in their favor.

I was going to do it.
I was going to jump.
I had to.

The whole world stopped when I jumped from reason
in the summer of '79.

They all signed my cast.
None called me chicken again.

FOREVER YOUNG

Intrepid youngster,
innocence is the substance
tainted in the man.

HUNGER AND DEFEAT

Every man should know hunger;
Every man should taste defeat:
Bread becomes satisfying,
And victory sweet.

DEATHLESS LOVE

I give you the light of my life
To hold it high for all the world to see;
To blind the ignorant with the knowledge
To resolve all things peacefully.
I also give you the darkness of my life:
My deepest humility.
I give my lessons so painfully learned
With my absence of sanctity.
Also hold these high for all the world to see,
For they aren't any less grand—
They teach a varied lesson
To those wise enough to seize the day at hand.
But of all the things I give to you,
There is one that will rise above,
And that is the gift of my eternally pledged,
Truthful, undying love.

RIGHTS

Right doesn't come without duty,
The two are inseparably tied.
If told you were owed a living,
I'm sorry, but somebody lied.

QUOD ERAT DEMONSTRANDUM

Of leaders past and present I've learned
That he serves best who is concerned—
Not with political destination—
But with the welfare of his nation.

IN SPITE OF PLASTIC FLOWERS
(And Other Cheapened Splendors of the World)

Pluck it from the ground.
Pluck it from the earth and tear away the beauty.
Rip it from the soil, hide it from the sun,
Shred off every petal, pull off every one.

Throw away the fragrant flower,
Piece by piece floating on the wind,
Drifting ever nearer to where it came,
Back to the earth that once its life sustained,
The beauty that it was and will be once again.

So go on, throw, throw it all away, every bit away—
Its perpetual beauty will be once more
In the merry month of May.

BEFORE IT'S TOO LATE

I will probably never tell you
all I have to say:
seasons change, tides turn,
the sun sets each fleeting day.
And though I yearn to share with you
every passing thought,
the years are wearing thin,
and time cannot be bought.

So before one of us holds
the hand of fate,
before precious time
has grown too late,
let me say, from me to you,
my dearest friend,
I love you.

I love you.

AMADEUS

Mathematic sounds:
instrumental harmony
that is razor sharp.

PASS SOON AWAY

There is a certain solitude
In every hour apart
That brings me to eternity
And breaks again my heart.

O let the firmament bestow
An azure burning bright!
Let the pinholes in the canvas
Shine spangled in the night!—

'Tis all in vain to cheer my heart
Or ease one bit the pain—
'Tis only when the one I love
Is in my arms again—

That I at last shall realize
The beauty of the day—
And come to find eternity
Passes too soon away.

REASON FOR REPENTANCE

The reason men repent is clear:
What stock of love for God they have
is simply second to their fear.

NO CIRCLE SO SOUND

No circle's so sound
That it's perfectly round;
No tool precise enough to measure.
No line's so exact
That it isn't abstract
Enough for a poetic pleasure.

THRESHOLD

My mind,

my boiling mind.

I shake its wings

to flush out its pulses of wisdom,

where clods cling to roots.

There's a part of knowing things

even the idle can squeeze

to let the music out.

I know out of nowhere,

degrees between desire

and the music

just out of reach:

a feather impossible to move.

INSULT TO INJURY

To quell the sanguine heart
When yours is torn apart
Brings company to share
The sting of Cupid's dart—

But doubling of the care
But doubles the despair—
Misery loves company
But finds no comfort there.

REMEMBERING CHILDHOOD

Perhaps I throw the stone into the lake
To see the circular ripples it makes
Roll toward the banks in miniature wakes.
Perhaps I throw the stone into the lake
To see the splashing disruption it makes
Measured by the number of fish it wakes.
Perhaps I throw the stone into the lake
For the sake of a drake and noise he makes
When he shakes like he aches upon the wakes.
Perhaps I throw the stone into the lake
To forsake the mistake that this man makes
When he doesn't partake of childhood wakes.

DAMN THIS SNOW!

Working in my garden today,
I cursed the heat I had longed for all winter.
My garden is pretty, though.
I water it with my sweat
each time I swipe at a gnat
I thought the frost had killed.
I hate particular people
and keep mostly to myself.
I think my neighbor's garden
is enough for both of us
and doubt I will keep one next year.

EMILY'S IN THE ATTIC

Emily's in the attic
With her clover and her bees,
Scratching out her poems
While standing on her knees.
Her secret love's at home
With a wife who doesn't please.
And Emily holds her breath
Writing please, please, please, please, please.

THE TOWN AN ETERNITY AWAY: A BOY ON A FARM

What memories of slow-rolling plains
Winnow the blanket of time from your recollection—
As the wind the chaff from the grain
In those very slow-rolling plains
You give resurrection?

Do you see thin smiles and vacant eyes
That yearn for dimples and a father's pride—
What are the memories of your youth?
Maybe you see a refulgent face
In an even brighter time and place—
Or perhaps time has distorted the truth?

> An empty silo leans to listen
> To the whispers of the fields
> That chase the wind—
> And a kite dances on a string
> In a hopeful sky—
> And you hold the string
> And sigh with the wind
> As no boy is meant—
> Listlessly—
> In the alienating fields
> Of your discontent.
> And somewhere a fence needs mending—
> Somewhere a sheep needs tending—
> Somewhere a boy is pretending
> He can fly away.

A MEAGER SEED

A meager seed
haphazardly strewn
by earth's collective sigh
pushes against itself
and struggles
to cleave the sky.

A pointed node
splits its coat
and thirsts for rain and shine,
snaking its way
instinctively—
and all with earth is fine.

A noiseless strain,
an immeasurable gain,
a subtle struggle to attain
its place among proud rings
and splendid things
and all that nobler than all kings:

The ascent begins
and the descent, too,
the roots grip
and the branches strew
themselves across the air,
and at last the eye is made aware
of a meager seed.

Y2K
(a parody of A. E. Housman's *When I was One-and-Twenty*)

When I was Y1K
   I heard my Mother say,
"Give days and weeks and years
   But not forever away;
Give minutes away and months
   But keep your future free."
But I was Y1K,
   No use to talk to me.

When I was Y1K
   Again I heard Her say,
"A thousand years are nothing
   If left as they were found;
But greed and neglect will ruin
   The air and sea and ground."
And I am Y2K,
   And oh, touché! touché!

O CHARLIE BOY

(Still lies the man so fast a boy:
His chest no longer fills nor falls;
His mother's heart's the devil's joy;
His father's pride the bugle calls.)

This final call I shall regret,
O Charlie Boy, dear friend of mine,
It's been so long since last we met
I scarcely can recall the time.

This is no time nor place to meet
For two friends so long departed,
And why these tears upon my feet,
And your mother broken-hearted?

You went off to be a sailor,
But you have returned without leave.
I'll lie for you, O Charlie Boy,
Though it be the stripes off my sleeve.

And when the bell of my life tolls
To mark the end of earthly joy,
I'll come to climb heavenly poles
With you, my friend, O Charlie Boy!

>In memory of Charles Brian Holiday
>June 1, 1969 — August 1, 1992

I'M IT

The spout not cooled splatters
water that won't be tea,
driblets that will not steep
for all eternity.

Your hands fumbled my youth
and memories became excuses,
but the finger of blame
has only negative uses.

Blame is that perpetual game of tag
that can only end when one finally says,
"Yes, you are right, I am it."

REGRETS

Seconds evolve into minutes;
minutes into hours—
neatly packed capsules of time
we have no choice but to swallow.
      I have devoured a lifetime.

I lick an empty plate
and beg for seconds.
But the cupboards are bare
and the seconds are gone.
I am still hungry.
      But I am done.

STRAPPED

Winter's charity dead,
the truth vomiting up the morning,
I imagine her wrapped in the wind,
her finger jammed down on me,
her minion coming to mark the spot.

I imagine the last stitch of the wind
sewn into the surface of her wrath.
Her laugh a fiendish howl
echoing through the desolate
expanse of her icy heart.

And there I am,
shivering in awe in spite of myself,
naked,
frozen,
a glutton strapped to her will.

HATEMONGERS

The mothers' treasured babes,
None of whom were born knaves,
Fratricide when they grow:
The babes learn hate,
The babes learn death,
The babes learn color after a breath.
And we wonder were they'll go—
And who put them there.

THE MEASURE OF SUCCESS

A fistful,
a wallet so thick
it's like sitting on a baseball—
it hurts.
But it's always there,
no matter what or how much—
name the price,
I'll take it.
So I sleep to dream.
What's a dream but reality admitted
to what consciousness denies,
refuses to acknowledge,
believe or accept?
Happiness?
How much is it?
I'll write a check.

DEPARTED FLOWER

I made your perfume from petals,
Beheading poppies all day,
Until I had a measure
Tampering with Nature's way.

We blew upon dandelions
To set their seedlings free,
To watch their fragile crowns
Impart fertility.

And in the spring, when I returned,
A host created new
Searched my mind for fragrances,
But no more poppies grew.

So I held a crown to my lips,
Kissed it as your face so pale,
Cried a tear and drew a breath,
And died waiting to exhale.

THE FINAL TOLL:
A FAREWELL TO LIBERTY

The idle minds that lusted
For the silence they trusted
Will no longer need to foist:
The bell not used has rusted;
Her throat is mute and busted;
Her message no longer voiced.

JUST A THOUGHT...

We live, as generations have and will,
in deep perpetual ignorance,
self-pity, hatred, jealousy, and greed.
We live as we have been taught:
by the example of the equally damned;
the equally ignorant.
We never quite stop being impressionable;
we never quite learn to think for ourselves—
not fully, not really.
And we will never be free
while history thinks for us.
Seemingly, we are forever lost
in the abysmal depths of blame.

BANISHED

Am I so banished from these dark walls
to never sleep here again?
I console and conciliate,
but no patriot I be
till much nobler causes compel the bloodshed of men!

So, soundly I'll sleep afar,
for I've not tasted the bitter consequence of guilt;
I've not trodden on white faces
or held a marker of a way
while shouting over gunfire some boastful cry
in the midst of the truth falsely called freedom,
only to have it sink in my stomach and burn my eyes
for I could not justify the dealing of last breaths!

Dear soldiers and lime-wearers,
sleep fast—
sleep fast and true—
hold remorse close.
Soil or feathers,
the make of your bed holds you
with eyes that open or eyes that don't—
it holds you in contempt in your homeland.
And, although I sleep in exile,
my conscience doesn't sleep in a nether world.

BE STILL, LILY

Two o'clock: time for a shake and a dribble.

I used to squeeze her hands,
two or three times a day,
trying to keep them still.

But Parkinson's grip was always stronger.

I wanted to shake it out of her!
I wanted to throw it away!
I wanted to be her hero,
not just her grandson.
I would have gladly shaken for her
and let her hate God
two or three times a day.

Looking back now I realize,
for that reason,
I was her hero.

Sweet dreams, Lily.
Sweet dreams.

PROMONTORY

This promontory has it over me
with its nurturing soil turned toward the sea
all day, every day,
in good weather and not:
its face on the water's edge;
its feet wading in the swells;
its arms collecting shells;
its stomach over a dredge;
its shoulders bare and hot
all day, every day,
in good weather and not—
unlike me,
a man
who can barely see to see
the sea in me.

FAINTING STEPS

He stumbles in,
legless and sweating gin.
I hear his thick hand
searching for the light,
and I pray he'll forget
where my room is.

He coughs,
scuffs the wall with a boot,
and chokes on his heavy tongue.
I feel sick
but try to keep still
and pretend to be asleep.

I can see his shadow
under my door—
paused, thinking,
then turning down the hallway.

My grip eases on the blanket,
and my heart slows
with each step fainter than his last.

THE TIME ON SOMEONE ELSE'S WATCH

Your face I've never seen
Your troubles I don't know
Your annoying tics
And idiosyncratic fits
Are yours and yours alone

All I see tonight's your hair
Your eyes and their alluring stare
All around is hushed and stilled
Your mother doesn't impose her will
And this arm in mine no pulse to thrill

And the tick on your wrist
Marks the sweat in my fist
How perfect you are from afar
And the hands go around
Because I haven't found
Out who you are

TWO SONS

Years ago
the monitor sounded,
as it sounds tonight:
The crib was wet,
two a.m.,
it was your turn.

The shrill cry that pierced my sleep
still echoes the damned recollection:
A limp and still six weeks of life
clutched against your chest,
I found you sitting on the floor
in the corner of his room,
rocking back and forth,
crying softly,
whispering a lullaby.

Tonight I say,
"I'll go."
You whisper,
"Let's go together."
We go,
and, oh, how his tears are bittersweet.

LAST CHRISTMAS

My woebegone friend,
who never had much luck
with work or women,
hunches over his sink,
his posture that of an
eighty-year-old Atlas
(the weight of the world
taking its toll),
the hot water running as
he washes last week's dishes.

"I just don't know," he says as
he tells me his latest hardship,
his newest unfortunate situation.
"I just don't know," he says again,
slowly and wastefully running
his uncalloused hands
over a soapy, slippery glass.

He goes on and on
about this and about that
for fifteen minutes or more,
the hot water now cold
still running from the tap.
"I need a bigger water heater," he says.

The glass slips from his hands,
shatters against the sink.
The dusty plug on the back of the basin
would slap him if it had hands.
"I just don't know."

"You're right about that," I say.
He doesn't hear me.
He never hears me.
I haven't said a word;
I'm tired of talking.
I grab my coat and leave.

Outside in the night air
I see him through a window,
still standing at his sink.
I shake my head,
the Christmas chill unbearable,
and wonder how he'll make it
through the night
with no hot water.

TON UPON TON UPON TON

It seemed so unthinkable
A ship dubbed "unsinkable"
Could ever submerge her deck—
Ton upon ton upon ton.

But the Titanic went down
In icy waters that drown
And the whole world mourned her wreck—
Ton upon ton upon ton.

The rescued few who returned
Two feet to the ground they yearned
Were welcomed by crowded shores—
Ton upon ton upon ton.

But the heft of Titanic—
The recall of the panic—
The salt in their captain's sores—
Ton upon ton upon ton.
Ton upon ton upon ton.

AFTER A HOUSE OF CARDS

When the chosen two-facedly forsake
Their choosers to build their own foundation,
Trumping ex cathedra those who partake
In the real building of this nation;
When in ruin our governing house lies—
The ace atop the king atop the queen—
What of the trusted flush that now belies
The many promises turned Byzantine?

A pyramid's power is its people,
The myriad bricks shouldering the weight;
While a strong wind may topple the steeple,
It pushes the faithful to vindicate—
Then a new spire, a phoenix from the shards,
Arises constructed of bricks, not cards.

THE LAST COWBOY

(On a winter day on the Colorado plains,
With the tumbleweeds and the Santa Fe trains,
People came to say good-bye,
'Cause his body was gone . . .
But his spirit won't die.)

Like the Indians my grandpa believed
That Nature gives but she also receives.
So we gave her his body and we gave her his soul;
We gave thanks to God and praised him for the loan.
But, O Lord, you've left us a debt we can't repay,
'Cause there ain't no way to measure a man so great.

He used to set me on his knee and call me Buck
As I steered through town in his pickup truck.
He was a lovin' man with a twinkle in his eye—
He used to get excited over pumpkin pie.
He told it like he saw it—he only knew the truth—
And there ain't a man alive who could ever fill his boots.

When I get to Heaven and earn my wings
We're gonna catch up on a lot of things.
We can leg wrestle and tell tall tales
'Bout Bonnie and Clyde and Josie Whales.
We can flex our muscles to see who's smaller
And sing songs all day and compare who's taller.

And I'll say "Grandpa, you're fibbin' to me—
There ain't no way you grew to six-foot-three!"
And you can smile and stretch your back,
Grab your ribs and tip your hat,

And then turn to me, like you always did,
And say "Now, Bucky, you know I can't fib."

And we'll laugh out loud until we cry,
Till ol' Saint Pete tells us to fly.
But until that day, grandpa, my friend,
I'll think of you till we're together again,
And cherish the memories I haven't outgrown
Of the only cowboy this kid's ever known.

    In memory of Clifford Hittle,
    my beloved grandfather

HALF YES, HALF NO, HALF STAY, HALF GO

Somewhere between hello and good-bye,
    I doubt . . .
For half in love with you am I,
    and half out.

THE DEEPEST SUFFERING

Loneliness is the deepest suffering I have ever known,
Far greater than a break or sprain or separated bone,
For these are only superficial and leave an outward scar,
But despair afflicts the inside, where the meanings are.

THE CHASM

The flash flood had turned cracks into ditches and ditches into gorges. You were precious, seven and badly wanting to play with your big brother. To be one of the guys you would have to leap a gorge. But your legs couldn't push quite as hard as you were being pushed. When your fragile little face smashed into the other side of that chasm, I thought you'd died. You, of course, were fine. I, however, am still very much injured.

AMERICA, AMERICA
(a 1980's Anthem of Reality)

America, America,
I hope God sheds his grace on us,
Because our streets are full of murder
And our children full of drugs.
And there is little good in our brotherhood—
From sea to polluted sea—
O dear, America,
I pray God sheds his grace on thee.

With our hazy brown mountain majesties
Above the poisoned plain;
Our lakes and rivers
Infested with acid rain—
O say! can't you see
In our children's bloodshot eyes
That our United States of America
Is slowly beginning to die?

From the halls of the drug pushers' mansions
To the porch of the working man's shack,
We're afraid to send our kids to school
Because of AIDS, guns, and crack.
Should we be proud to be Americans,
In the land of the free(?) and the home of the knave—
Or should we take the Star Spangled Banner
And bury it in its grave?

It's time that Americans took a stand;
Loved their neighbors and held their hands.
Instead of wallowing in selfish pity

We should be cleaning up our cities.
Just open your eyes, it's not hard to see,
And pray God sheds his grace on thee.
America, America,
I pray God sheds his grace on thee.

A POCKED ELLIPSE

(Absorbing victory,
the sun, aggressive—indeed, pounding—
claimed with justification
order to the vast wind
blowing away the twentieth century.)

The mental bullshit.
The satellites.
The bloody banks.
The well-intentioned men wedded to currency.
Out of touch with feeling.
"It's bad economics."
The gatekeeper has always made our system open.
We are delighted to sell it to anybody.
It is rubbish—all rubbish!
We have no deals.
What deals could we do?

The warnings couldn't be clearer,
but the empire stretches
to new radical forms of fascination.
The cities rise.
We all bow down and let buggers get away with murder.
So, paused again in the flinty sunlight of the times,
the empire intact,
clinging to the status quo,
we wait for the next wind.

KANSAS LOVES COMPANY
(THE YEAR I DIDN'T VISIT HOME)

After brother called,
depressed, even forlorn,
going home in July—
Kansas lifting murderous noons
of parched, quenchless, relentless suns—
to undertake vicarious worrying,
xerographic yesterdays zeroed.

ACCOUNTABLE

Stunted by your apathy
and selfish agenda,
I was a seed in your shadow,
able to grow only when I shined
the spotlight of negative attention
upon myself.

Yes, I was a trouble maker.
But your hands fumbled my youth
and memories became excuses,
but the finger of blame I pointed
was a mirror of futile uses.

The finger points back at me.
I stand accountable.

APOCALYPTIC REVERSAL

I will pillage,
I will squander,
I'll waste it all
While Hell grows fonder—

I will not give,
I'll only take,
For I am War,
And Heaven's too late!

FALLING APART

She asks me where I've been
(*Nowhere* is not a place).
I smile when I'm nervous:
My lips crack, cold and chapped;
Guilt frozen on my face.

She smells my cloak and wants to know
Who's breaking up our home.
I slump in a squalor
With red cheek and collar,
And yellow in every bone.

She glowers but I can't shrug;
Guilt's gravity has a greater tug.
My tongue stumbles.
My spine crumbles.
She sweeps me under the rug.

HARD HABITS TO BREAK

Cracked,
egg-shell brown,
yolk-stained looking fingers—
a permanent yellow no soap could remove.

He couldn't give them up:
five packs a day,
a carton in two,
700 cigarettes a week.
I've done the math,
calculated every puff—
over 60,000 a month for 38 years—
all those tainted inhalations!

I called him Black Lung,
the pale-faced Indian
whose peacepipe had a filter
and a government warning.

Then a slip at fifty-six
on a bar of soap in the tub
snapped his neck.
His life snuffed out,
we found him:
stone-cold
water splashing on his chest;
his water-logged, ghostly-white skin
a canvas for the yellow hands
resting on his belly.

And now my sister,
at thirty-two,
diagnosed with cancer.
She, who never had a puff,
is given a year to live.
And the only advice I can give her:
Beware of soap bars on bathtub floors.

A UNIQUE FLOWER

My mama was a funky diva
When I was growing up,
She found her voice at night
At the bottom of a whiskey cup.

From impaired nocturnal blossomings
Came my mama's power,
But I know now that rain
Can drown even the strongest flower.

My father and she were quite a match
Made after they made me,
The seed carelessly strewn
In the garden of their apathy.

I see her now in a photograph
And taste the whiskey sour,
Awestruck by the beauty
Of such a strange yet splendid flower.

A PARENT'S PRAYER FOR A CHILD SOLDIER

My soldier boy, so fresh from school,
My know-it-all turned into fool—

Overnight from a peaceful quad
To a field of a lesser god—

Shoot straight, son, straight and true,
Live to see tomorrow through—

And someday soon to your home come
To hear me say, "I love you, son."

SHE SAID GOOD-BYE

If today is a gift
because its called the present,
I wonder if I can return
the gift I got yesterday—
just take it back
like some unwearable tie
Picasso painted after a fight
with a fifth of gin?

But there it is,
with its thumbs in its ears,
fingers waiving,
its tongue sticking out at me,
the sign that reads
NO RETURNS OR EXCHANGES.
So I thrust it deep into my pocket,
yesterday, that is,
and head home.

On the highway I debate
throwing it out the window,
but the state trooper in my rearview
and the NO LITTERING signs
keep my windows up.

At home I contemplate . . .
the lawnmower, the garbage disposal,
the toilet . . . I'll flush it away!
But flush after flush it's unsinkable,
bobbing back with each burp of the bowl.
I pull it out, not bothering to dry it off,

and make my way to the kitchen.

On the butcher's block
I hack and pound and saw at it.
But it's impenetrable,
inaccessible,
sealed like some ancient tomb
containing the secrets of a lost world
no one can relive—
one can only imagine how things
might have been.

BURN VICTIM

Ice-divided panes
tingle in bursts
of glazing light
to a point beyond
the lightest touch—

Sizzling on my fingertips—
like blood into the flame—
boiling in my heart—
your face within a frame—
and nothing more.

SEPARATION

In my bedroom beneath the kitchen,
while I listened to the joists creak as you paced above,
I strained to hear the words you shouted at each other
during your midnight arguments.

The joists have long since stopped creaking,
and I realize now that our house was not old,
just poorly constructed.

POISONED SEEDS:
THE WAIF, THE WHORE, THE SOCIETY

The waif I needn't know
To know of his despair—
He builds a futile fire
Under a wooden chair.
I've sat in the hot seat,
Been burned without a care,
Wondered where my home was
And wished that I were there.

The whore she doesn't show
Emotion for her fare—
Her life is all to dire
And can't afford the wear.
I've peddled on the beat,
Stolen without a care,
Wondered where my pride was
And by loss made aware.

The waif and whore are seeds
In a fruitless soil,
Drowning in a deluge
Of a failing toil.
I've drowned in selfish needs,
Caused my blood to boil,
And then searched for refuge
From that which I spoil.

The waif, the whore, and I
Are similar, you see,
For they are both dying,
And I am their disease.

THOUGHT UPON SEEING A BAREFOOT BOY

I have heard stories about corpses,
people who were laid to rest
with hair barely touching their collars,
years later exhumed and found
with hair down to their toes,
where their nails, once neatly trimmed,
now push through their wasted shoes.

DERAILED TRAIN OF THOUGHT

Six A.M. and the train
again is my wake-up call.
The god-awful clamor,
as I rise and stammer
my "good morning" to the wall,
rattles the dusty pane
where my reflection hangs
in a broken frame of mind.

My molars grind.
The plumbing clangs.
The tub fills with rusty rain.
6:10 and the train again
has derailed my train of thought.

A VOICE FOR CHANGE

I walked amidst a plane of pestilence,
A level of consciousness paralyzed by ignorance,
And from soul to soul—if souls be souls—
The essence of each I walked among was naught.
Though all around was gilded bright,
Adorned with fortunes of vain-laborious days,
And though the streets shone so bright
With ornaments of appetite,
The being of each contained within was poisoned.
And the children of the day—seduced!
Unsuspecting youth—corrupted!
Their innocence defeated—thwarted by society's fashion!
And I stood on the vast expanse of space and time
With visions of good intent—
With but my voice as my implement.

SLANT

Kill me not with slanted word
Or privy incidental—
Stab your huff into my back,
Though it be detrimental,
For I'd rather die a death
Full of privileged life I've spent
Than to live a life of death
Through the truth that you have bent.

SHADOWS AND AFRICAN AMERICANS

Black, stretch with the sun—
stretch into oblivion—
then become the night.

HOOKER

Her alabaster breasts
Purposely pressed
Together rise proudly
Against full lungs
For many a man to marvel—

A tight leather mini
Shows symmetry
Apportioned perfectly
Where two sleek legs
Of marble stretch infinitely—

She plants a hollow kiss
With scarlet lips
Against her fingertips
And wafts with breath
Akin to death a mortal bliss—

Compensated lover
Of another—
Metamorphic mother
Under cover
In the passages of darkness.

I KNOW THAT ONE

Tears smear black and white
into a shade of gray. Damn!
Obituaries.

INTERLUDE FOR RELIGION

Consecrated church of yore:
Dilapidated; hence, no more.
Pews, all perfect in a row:
Long-vacant, pretty, though.
Crucifix, high over the altar:
Thorns, deeper; doesn't falter.
Rosary! rosary! get to a station,
For it is time for the last damnation!
Ah! the sinners, all shall be,
Perishing here for eternity
To take away the sins of the earth;
To have at last their holy mirth—
Until soon after, with frustration,
Some fool gives in to temptation
And lets religion resurrect its flank
And laugh for millenniums
All the way to the bank.

RECOVERING

A man swallows hard.
Beads of sweat form on his brow.
No alcohol now.

I SEE THE SEA NO MORE

My clothes fly fired skies,
and I am not in them.
I am gently rocking over waves:
naked body floating, air trapped, I am dead.
My tired eyes at last closed.
My body belongs to the ocean.
The seawater surges though my ears.
The fish swim in my head.

I think I see the Titanic,
And seaweed waving to me.
The ocean takes my breath away:
human airless dead sink like lead.
The current is like a friend, though,
bringing food to others.
Lifeless, I didn't dread
being tasteful to the shark I fed.

I HATE COLORS

I conciliate my feelings;
push dark thoughts aside—
still I cannot kindle compassion
for men whose eyes are deep pools of hatred,
men whose eyes see every color
and hold each varied shade with unequal worth.

I can distinguish the hues of the rainbow,
but from man to man, as it should be,
I am color-blind.

AT THE CONVENTION OF PAST TYRANTS AND GENERALS

This is a big day in Heaven.
The Halo Dome is packed to capacity,
the turnstiles littered with feathers and golden chits.
Vendors fly up and down the aisles,
Get your tablets! loaves! fishes!
The air is aflutter with angels flying to and from the bathrooms.
The energy is palpable.

The P.A. booms: *Please take your perches.*
The convention will begin in five minutes.
No one looks for a clock, there are none.
After all, this is Heaven, and time's irrelevant.

Ladies and gentlemen, the P.A. booms again,
Welcome to the Halo Dome and the six thousandth
Convention of Past Tyrants and Generals.
Please join me in singing God Bless Heaven,
Led by the incomparable Elvis Presley.

The convention erupts as Elvis (on loan from Hell),
dressed in a platinum jumpsuit with sequined wings,
enters though an enormous purple curtain on the main stage.

It is estimated that 4,126,000,000 people died during the
twentieth century from all causes. Manmade deaths accounted
for approximately 185,000,000 of these. That means that one out
of every twenty-two deaths was manmade.

God, I hope my alarm doesn't go off. This should be one hell of
a conference.

SWEET SACHET

O sachet let out grandma's smell,
The light catches its shape so well:
I see her face in the filtered powder,
From smiles to screams as the sun grows louder.
Let me remember her once more,
The perfumed lady I adore—
Just one last taste of her bouquet
And then I'll put you both away,
Save the memory for another day.
Back to the vanity, my sweet sachet.

WHAT SUBTERFUGE IS THIS, O HEART

What subterfuge is this, O heart?
You conjure up your own denial
Of happiness with increasing toll,
And waste away each caring part
With resonating spasmodic guile!
It is not the sounding of the soul!
Just the pangs of a hungry heart!

RAPETURE

She feels his dank thrusts,
hears the beast scream.
A mephitic steaming stream
seeps through her knots.

Rude. Quick. Lunatic.
She falls into a muck of waste—
gags, cries, and begins to rot.

*Every two minutes another woman is
raped in the United States—a grotesque
and animal-like violation that may seem
like a rapture to the perpetrator, but is a
living hell for the victim.*

TEACH THE CHILDREN WELL

Every day a blackened soul,
A diamond turned back into coal,
Fuels the fire of lessons untold
And burns the truth while flames unfold
Around the naked innocence
Of ignorance and indolence—
So teach the children well.

ZEBRAS IN THE ATTIC

Once the clouds were unattainable;
Now the moon has been done before.
Between these slits of light and dark—
These zebras on the floor—
I wonder what all this conquering's for.

ROTTEN MILK

The baby sits—
pacified, rapt, hypnotized—
spoon-fed by its mother.
A thirsty sponge—
insatiable—
the baby soaks it in,
swallows the sustenance of
culture, spits out nothing.

Dissatisfied, desensitized—
the nipple raw and swollen—
the baby wails for more and more—
knows which buttons to push.
The mother never falls asleep.
She obliges, coming across
with nipple after nipple
at any hour of the day or night.
The baby switches at will,
instantly satisfied or dissatisfied
with its inexhaustible supply
of rotten milk.

DISGUSTED

Packed my things today—
just stuffed 'em in a case—
had enough of mankind—
enough of this damned place.
Closed my accounts—
withdrew every cent—
boarded up the windows—
paid my last month's rent.

I'm ready to go.
So I walk to the station—
the tracks have but one plane
and the planes one atmosphere—
can't find a vehicle
to get me outta here.
Nobody's goin' my way.
I just say God damn it!
didn't you hear the news today?
Time to move to another planet.

THE CLOSING

A clammy handshake,
a closing of a deal—
not the union of two hearts
but the consolidation of two accounts.
The perfunctory rings,
the dress with the receipt saved,
the ceremonial meeting—
a social endeavor
for our separate friends
who secretly warned us:
marriage is forever,
not just a tax break.
"You may kiss good-bye."

ONE RACE: HUMAN

Kaleidoscope, spin your colors,
glance the light into a thousands prisms,
then tell me: Does one color outshine another?
Is one more brilliant than the next?

Kaleidoscope, your truth is spun,
one color is less without another.
Less radiant. Less vivid. Less beautiful.
No one would peer though you
to view a single, solitary shade.
It is each hue combined
that creates the beauty of the whole.
Detract or increase and all is diminished.

PACKS

She has only one lung . . .
    it is failing.
The other . . .
    in a petri dish—
a thousand petri dishes—
some over-important medical student
peering down a scope—
"So that's lung cancer, eh?"

The Surgeon General snickers
behind his little white coat—
"I told you so, you dummy.
Can't you read?"

Shut up, asshole!
Fix it and give it back!

FRUSTRATION

You persistent, pestering mosquito,
Oh, how you try my countenance!
You are neither brave nor stupid;
In fact, you are nothing but a nuisance!

(do not bite me)

If 'twere another time I mightn't care,
But the hand is upon the hour
When I'm looking to pen my rhyme;
Therefore, I am apt to commit a crime.

(do not make me)

I'll pulverize your body with this rock!
With all my daily frustration
I shall squash you into a spot
Out of the anger of things I am not!

(but want to be)

STARVING THE CROWS

Crow \kro\ noun: any of several large oscine birds of the genus Corvus, of the family Corvidae, having a long, stout bill, lustrous black plumage, and a fan-shaped tail.

Scavenger \ska-ven-jer\ noun: an animal or other organism that feeds habitually on refuse or carrion.

NOTICE

> Please seal your trash containers tightly. Crows, seagulls and other scavengers are making trash collection unnecessarily difficult and time consuming.
>
> Thank you for your cooperation.

Everyone in my neighborhood received the notice. It was straightforward and made complete sense: scavengers were making a general mess of things on trash day; do your part to help make the job a little easier. It seemed simple enough.

Thursday is trash day in my neighborhood, and most put theirs out on Wednesday night for the early morning pickup. It's kind of a ritual around my house. Wednesday evening, usually just after supper, I reluctantly start collecting the trash from around the house. There seems to be a preset order to this ho-hum process. First, I go upstairs and gather the trash from under the bathroom sink and from the small wastebasket in the master bedroom's walk-in closet. Then, with trash in hand, I go downstairs for three more pickups: the kitchen closet, under the kitchen sink, and then the second bathroom. I leave everything I've collected so far by the door to the garage, and then go down into the basement, where my desk is, and collect the last of the trash from the basket under it. At every stop I make, except for those where the only trash allowed is paper and the like, I secure another liner in the bin.

At the point when all of the garbage throughout the house is collected, the job is about half done. I then proceed to load all of the trash into two large garbage barrels I keep in the garage. The two barrels are usually sufficient to hold all of the trash my family produces, except perhaps after holidays and the occasional party. With the garage door open, I get on with schlepping the heavy barrels one at a time to the end of my driveway, where they remain overnight for pickup the following morning. I trudge back up the drive, close the garage door, and go back inside the house, usually feeling an overriding sense of relief that this utterly mundane chore is over for another week. Actually, it's more of an assignment than a chore. My wife, who does practically every other job around the house, has mandated that the taking out of trash will be the one task I'm to complete without question. And I do, albeit with the alacrity of an inmate sentenced to a life of busting rocks in a prison yard.

~

I've had a general fascination with crows and ravens for as long as I can remember. They're such alluringly resourceful and resilient creatures. There's a certain mystique about them that I've been strangely drawn to throughout my life. Perhaps it's because of their ability to survive and indeed thrive under harsh conditions that they receive so much of my consideration. Perhaps it's because they've been vilified and made the personification of evil by such writers as Shakespeare, Hitchcock, Poe, and scores of others, including in such early literary works as Beowulf, that I venerate their toughness. Perhaps my admiration towards them is because they embody in their innocence the attributes so like those I wish I had. Perhaps it's all of this and much more. Whatever the reason, I find the adaptable, intelligent and enchanting creatures not otherworldly and evil but laudable and even loveable.

In spite of my high regard for crows and ravens, however, I didn't give them a second thought upon reading the notice I received from the city. I found the bright yellow sheet of paper with its message shouting at me in bold black letters jammed between my front door and my screen door. Yes, I nodded in agreement as I read the appeal, the streets were generally a mess on trash day. Asking people to seal their trash containers tightly was responsible and appropriate. In short, I didn't bat an eye when I read the notice. If cleaning up the neighborhood was needed, then I was going to do my part.

~

I was glad to see on the first Thursday morning following the notice that most all my neighbors had answered the call for help. Their cooperation and consideration was evident when I turned the corner onto Jenkin's Road on my way to work. Both sides of the street were neatly lined with tightly sealed garbage containers stretching all the way to North Street, a distance of just over a mile. I felt a sense of pride and appreciation as I drove past these miniature pillars of cooperation. I was glad to live in a neighborhood such as this. Perhaps taking out the trash would become less of a chore and more of a contribution to the efforts of my city. I could feel like I was really helping a worthwhile cause.

Everything went well for the first few weeks following receipt of the notice. Thursday would come, I'd go to work, and on my drive in I'd notice the efforts of like-minded neighbors doing their part to support the city's efforts to make trash collection easier. But I noticed something else, too. I noticed one morning that a large murder of crows (another vilifying term) seemed to be somewhat subdued and even a little confused. "What in tarnation is going on?" I could almost hear them ask. "Have these people all gone batty?"

I watched the crows with great scrutiny over the ensuing weeks and noticed subtle changes in their behavior. It seemed they were fighting amongst themselves, which perhaps wouldn't be too unusual if there were even a crumb between them, but there wasn't. I found that their behavior disturbed me, and I began to wonder if my neighbors and I had influenced their behavior by barring them access to our garbage.

The crows were in my thoughts more often as the cold winter weeks of Maine in January inched closer to better weather. I even had a strange dream one night in which a single crow implored me to open my refrigerator so that it could snack on a half-eaten sandwich I hadn't finished at lunchtime. It was all very strange. Here I was, a perfectly logical and rational man, finding myself thinking regularly about the crows. Where did they sleep? Were they freezing to death? Were they starving to death? I couldn't get them out of mind.

~

On a cold Thursday morning six or seven weeks after the city had asked earnestly for help, something surreal and dreamlike happened when I left my house for work. At the end of my driveway, perched atop one of my two garbage barrels was a large black crow that seemed to be staring at me as I approached my car, which I had moved out of the garage the night before to make gathering the garbage easier. I hadn't bothered to put it back.

Not being the superstitious type, I stared back at the crow as I fumbled with my keys to unlock the car door. It was a beautiful bird whose sable plumage seemed slicked-back and unctuous under the rays of the early February sun. Wise-looking and stalwart, like a centurion guarding the meaning of life, it stood unflinchingly still as its eyes mesmerized my own. This was no devious and fiendish fowl deserving of such a condemning and malevolent reputation as the one mankind has placed upon it. The bird, although cunning, was not evil.

I stared at the bird for a few seconds longer, still thinking about how those who don't understand it have maligned it for centuries. A chill came over me and I shivered abruptly, waking myself from my thoughts of the bird.

Shaking off the chill, I turned to unlock my car door and in so doing turned my back to the crow. I had no sooner averted my eyes when it let out a single attention-demanding caw. Slightly startled, I turned back towards it. It hadn't moved.

"What?" I said aloud to my beady-eyed visitor, not expecting a response but speaking more out of repartee than anything. "How can I help you this morning?" I laughed inwardly at my silliness and turned back to the car. Just as I did, though, much to my surprise, the crow let out another single caw. I turned again.

"What?" I asked, this time gesticulating with my arms out and my palms turned upward, again not expecting a response but instead having fun with the peculiar situation. "I can't help you if you don't talk to me."

Standing there with my arms out it dawned on me that if my neighbors were watching they'd think me half mad for talking to a crow, especially in the emphatic way I was doing so. I pretended to stretch, reaching towards the sky while I subtly scanned my neighbors' doors and windows. Satisfied that no one was watching, I turned back to my car.

Just as I went to insert the key into the lock, I could barely believe my ears when I heard the crow caw at me again. "You are a persistent little creature, aren't you?" I said, attempting not to move my lips as I turned to face the crow for the third time. This time, however, while looking straight at me, my vociferous visitor let out a fourth caw. What happened next is one of the most amazing things I've ever seen.

~

From where I was standing, the crow was approximately twenty feet away, which seemed a comfortable distance, although I did think it would be a rare occasion for a human to get much closer to a wild animal, especially a bird. From this distance, I didn't feel threatened or threatening, I could see the crow clearly, and I decided that it clearly wanted something. As I stood there, wondering what it was exactly this little black beauty wanted, it crouched slightly and sprang forward from the barrel. Its wings shot out and made a sort of half-flap before landing about a foot in front of the garbage barrel. Strangely, in spite of our proximity to one another, I wasn't in the least bit afraid.

The crow and I stared at each other intently, each of us intrigued by the other. The bird tipped its head to the right, back to center, and then back to the right where it held the position for a few seconds before returning to center. The behavior reminded me of my dog when he becomes curious about something. I thought the gesture a sign of intelligence, as if the bird was trying to figure me out, trying to see what made me tick, or trying perhaps to size me up. The crow then hopped forward. Then forward again. "Okay," I thought, "what are you doing? You're getting a little too close for comfort."

The crow hopped forward a third time, undaunted by the shrinking distance between us. "Nice birdie," I said shakily, "let's not do anything crazy." It hopped forward again, apparently ignoring my suggestion that it not do anything crazy. After a fourth and then a fifth hop, with the distance between us down to about fifteen feet, the crow let out three sharp and startling caws. "Oh boy," I worried, "Hitchcock was right; the bird's calling for backup." But it wasn't, and none came.

How was I going to unlock and get into the car before this apparently deranged creature pecked my eyes out? I didn't need to answer the question, because as soon as I had formed it the crow hopped backwards twice, paused, then backwards twice more. Eased by the more comfortable space between us, I inhaled slowly and deeply before sharply exhaling my relief in a mist upon the cold morning air. The crow cawed again.

At this point it seemed I'd been standing there with the crow for about an hour, although in reality it was probably more like three or four minutes. I had to get going, it was cold and I still needed to defrost the windshield. The crow, however, had other plans.

Until you've seen a crow spread its wings, hop up and down in circles and caw like mad, you'll have just a faint idea of the effect this display had on me when I saw it. I concluded that the bird had to be ill or something. What other reason could there be for such a maniacal and frenzied demonstration? It was loud, too. A crow's caw can be heard for hundreds of yards, I was twenty feet away, and with all the commotion I thought it would be a good time to unlock the car and hop inside. I turned quickly to insert the key, but the crow stopped. It stopped completely. "And where do you think you're going?" I thought I heard it ask when I looked back at it. "Ugh, nowhere," would have come my reply if I hadn't thought my imagination was beginning to get the best of me.

With a single hop, the crow landed within an inch or two of the barrel upon which it had been perched earlier. It looked at me, cawed, and then turned back towards the barrel. It then looked back at me, almost as if it wanted to make sure that I was still watching, turned back to the barrel and in an instant began to peck violently at the thick plastic container. I was astonished. The crow stopped, hopped a quarter turn towards me, cawed, and then turned back to the barrel, which it continued to peck at with the intensity of a jackhammer.

This process repeated itself three or four times. I don't remember exactly how many times, because being thoroughly mesmerized by something makes you tend to forget the details. However, regardless of how many times the crow repeated this bizarre and strikingly odd act of cawing and pecking, it hit me, as if the crow's beak itself had split my mind open to receive the message I was supposed to hear: "I am hungry, remove the lids from these barrels and stop the insanity so that I can eat."

The crow was communicating with me, telling me precisely what it wanted. It was I, with this huge human brain, who took so long to understand its simple message. I who felt doubly ridiculous, first because it took me so long to see what it was the crow was trying to tell me, and then because I hadn't realized earlier that by sealing my garbage containers I was in fact starving the crows. I was starving the same animal whose dependency upon garbage I, and millennia of humans before me, had helped create. It didn't seem right.

Perhaps crows used to feed exclusively on carrion, long before the existence of man, but I knew that was not the case today. Crows still eat carrion, yes, but much of their food intake comes from the wasted morsels of men and women around the globe. I realized this, and I knew that I had to do something about it. I couldn't provide for a species and then rip the proverbial rug out from under its feet. I knew what I had to do. I had realized, as they say, an epiphany.

~

At certain times in a man's life he realizes that he's about to do something that he might regret in the future. But he does it anyway. Perhaps with apprehension, but he does it anyway. As I stood there on that cold February morning, I felt that I was about to commit such an act. Many men cower from the repercussions of not conforming to popular thinking, but I felt that what I was about to do was right and appropriate, even if my neighbors wouldn't understand or especially like it. The crows needed my help, and I had the good sense to give it to them.

I took one step towards the crow, which caused it to stop its commotion instantly. I took another and then another, moving slowly and cautiously, not out of trepidation but out of concern that I'd startle my ebony guest. I took a few more steps, pausing briefly between each one to assess the crow's comfort level, and my own for that matter. Although fixed intently on my every move, the crow seemed fine, and so did I.

I was now within just a step or two of the barrel and the bird, an unusually close distance for a man and a wild animal, but there we were, each of us in uncharted territory, the crow now looking nearly straight up at me and I directly down on it. I must admit that I felt somewhat distinguished and privileged. There I was, an ordinary man, apparently singled out, chosen by this beautiful creature to share in its mystique and splendor. I felt humble, trustworthy and genuine, willing to give wholly my deference to an animal not tainted by the many perversions of mankind. The longer I stood there, the more I wanted to help my feathered friend—whatever that meant and in whatever way I could.

Another slow step forward and I was within two feet of the crow. I was astonished, overwhelmed with amazement and curiosity. What was happening? The crow was unflappable, standing there with its wide-open eyes anchored to mine. "Go ahead, you know what you have to do." The bird may as well have pecked out the message in Morse code upon my forehead. But it didn't have to. It was all there in its eyes. The message was clear.

"Okay, little buddy, I hope you know what you're doing." With that, I reached out, took hold of the lid, removed it, and placed it atop the other barrel. That was it. That was all.

As soon as I set the lid down, the crow hopped back and spread its wings. It then began to stand on one leg and then the other in quick succession, waddling back and forth, turning in circles, cawing like crazy. I began to laugh. I couldn't control myself. The bird was dancing! It was dancing out of happiness and appreciation! They say that one man's junk is another man's treasure. Well, this crow had struck the mother lode, and I had provided the shovel!

~

The crow eventually stopped its dance and I left for work and left the crow to its feast. I never told anybody about the incident, and it wasn't long before most of the neighborhood was back to leaving its garbage uncovered. I never covered mine again. In fact, I threw the lids away.

I'm still waiting for the second notice; I'm glad the first one came, because I'll never forget the amazing events of that cold February morning when a hungry crow changed my life forever.

SYLLABLE COUNTER

What am I but a syllable-counter
In a land of jaded places—
A question between the sun and the moon
In a sea of haggard faces?

IRONY FINDS ME IN THE LIBRARY

In the silent library,
the book-filled library,
where dust is more prevalent than sound,
where your heartbeat and your conscience
can usually be found,
I came across an example
of man's duality,
a prime illustration
of our peculiarity:
on one wall,
a poster of fighting men;
on another,
Gandhi.
Irony finds me again,
in the silent library.

SUICIDE: A PERMANENT SOLUTION TO A TEMPORARY PROBLEM

Troubles are passing
and soon you will be laughing . . .
unless you are dead.

DIVORCE COURT

The crowd thins　　　　　　　and
　　the body language
becomes evident.　　They stand
　　　　　　　　　They glower
　　　　　　　　　　　　They nod
　　　and
in　　hostile bunches
　　　　　　　　as time draws near
　　　　　like　　　birds of prey
　　　　　　　they deploy　　　their
　　　　　　　　indignant　　touch
　　　　　　　　　until
they achieve an　　　uneasy
　　　　　　　　tally for the day
　　　　You have to pay for
　　　　　　　　killing
　　　　　　　　　　she has paid
and
　　　　　　　she figures　　　　　at
least one
　　　　　touching display of faith
　　　is　　　　payment
　　　　enough.

HELPLESS

Can't see the bottom.
Can't reach the top.
Can't touch the sides.

VOYAGE

A long way to the moon on a ferry
A long way for me and for Mary
A long way to understanding
Why the past's so demanding
One's life from the other
One son, one mother
One disregard
One facade
I'll sail
Home

SHRINKING BACKYARD

This twelve-year-old is lost;
that one, equally lost—his shepherd.
A flock of shepherdless shepherds.
Those, over there,
to your left and your right,
in front and behind you—lost.
What, you can't see them?

Statistics.
Slivers on a piechart.
Between the scores and the forecast,
a what-a-shame moment on the ten o'clock news.

Don't worry, you don't need to do a thing.
Don't even move.
They're coming for you.

THE MOURNING AFTER

When he died,
the calendar set out—unexpectedly—
(he strayed from religious practice)
mourning, observance,
a rigorous process—
morning, afternoon, evening—
some ancient obligation to his mother—
a difficult promise to keep.

The son, acquitted,
vindicated in the father—
the mourner—
mourning undertaken on behalf
of martyred parents—
murdered by the obscene day.

The results, dizzying—
the blows of the funeral—
formal, black, a shovel
stabbing at a mound of dirt,
a coffin thudding into a pit—
shaking, shaking, shaking grief and relief.

JERK BLUES

Sittin' on a park bench
readin' the paper,
checkin' out the low fares
to Jamaica.
Thumbin' through the obits—
a friend of mine—oh, shit!
Gotta change of plan,
gotta change of venue—
I won't be checkin' out
that jerk spice menu.

DEATH

A murder of crows
at midnight in December
cawing on the wind.

MONDAY MOURNING

They say if you hit
when you're falling in your sleep
you never wake up.

GRANDPA'S HANDS

Grandpa's hands were old and twisted,
like a knar on an old oak tree.
Not much good for doing manual things,
but oh they were a sight to see.
They told a story in themselves,
one man's life and how he lived it.
They were sometimes gentle,
they were sometimes hard,
but there was never a time
when they weren't loving.
I miss those hands.
I miss them a lot.

A CAROUSEL OF DAYS

I wonder if ever I'll change my ways
And be the man I thought I'd be
Upon this carousel of days?

Yet round and round the globe does blaze
As though it has some place to be.
I wonder if ever I'll change my ways?

Perhaps this spinning is merely some craze
From which in time I will be free
Upon this carousel of days?

Yet I grow dizzy in this maze
From which I know I should be free.
I wonder if ever I'll change my ways?

Perhaps this spinning is merely some phase
And waiting it out is the key
Upon this carousel of days?

But my back aches and my hair grays
And answers the question I always raise:
I wonder if ever I'll change my ways
Upon this carousel of days?

A CASE FOR WILLN'T

It doesn't mean they won't when they can't or they don't;
It wasn't that they wouldn't when they shouldn't or they couldn't;
They aren't and it isn't that they haven't when they didn't, they don't—
And that's why will should be willn't, and not won't!

A DEAD SOLDIER SPEAKS

"Learn it well.
Breathe it in and hold it in your lungs.
Do not keep the stench of death from your nose.
The mutilation is real.
It is not a figment of your imagination.
Share it with your family.
Too many are in denial
of the vultures pecking at my eyes
and the flies feeding on my putrid flesh.
Do not turn away in repulsion.
Too many have turned away already.
You need to see this.
You need to be haunted by this.
Do not hide your eyes from the maggots
crawling out of my mouth.
They have something to say.
They are talking to you.
Are you listening?
Is anybody listening?"

A FLY FORETELLS OF WINTER

Late fall and the fly is fat.
With a sputtering engine,
it lumbers though the heavy air of the kitchen,
punch-drunk from a season's fact of glass
and its own insatiable appetite;
winging without a destination
upon the cusp of death,
like a pilot out of fuel,
spiraling to an imminent end,
an imminent beginning.

A FRIEND'S ATTENTION

It is the eve of Thanksgiving,
and I am thankful for imperfection,
thankful that I am not always right,
not always the one with the best idea,
the best way.
I am grateful, too, that my closest friends,
when uncovering my error or hearing my misstatement,
revel with delight in the satisfaction of correcting me.
I am thankful for my neediness,
no matter how much I pretend it isn't there.

A LITTLE MADNESS

Madness, that explosion of dormancy,
Rises like lava in unheeding eyes,
Like tides churning in the calm of the sea
Later flung upon ships in half-surprise.
To think no madness is madness utter—
Though an atom's split if you foster it
Long in the sore-speaking heart aflutter
So ignored by the senses spurning it.
Like the numbing effects of alcohol,
Which intoxicate our trained deportment,
A little madness comes over us all
In an ether-like rainbow assortment:
    'Tis not when but how we answer the call,
    For a little madness comes to us all.

A NEW WEIGHT-LOSS PROGRAM

OPENER:

If you're like a lot of Americans then you're tired of hearing about crazy fad diets with outrageous claims about losing tons of weight in just a short time. You're sick of hearing about miracle pills that burn off your excess fat while you sleep. Well, like you, I too am tired of hearing high protein, low carbohydrate; 30 pounds in 30 days; a shake with every meal; one pill with two glasses of water; eggs only; veggies only; blah, blah, blah! That's why I've created an all-new and completely revolutionary weight-loss program. Introducing *Exercise!* Developed during the Prefastfood and Pretelevision eras, this amazing program has helped people just like you shed zillions of unwanted pounds—that's zillions with a Z! What's best about *Exercise!* is that there's absolutely nothing to buy! That's right, *Exercise!* won't cost you a penny! A never-ending supply of *Exercise!* can be found right inside your own body! Look no further than the edge of your couch! All you have to do is get off your ass NOW!

DISCLAIMER:

The *Exercise!* program is most effective when you actually use it. A certain amount of effort and energy is required for the *Exercise!* program to work. *Exercise!* is not for everyone, only those who can get off their backsides and do something about their condition. *Exercise!* is also more effective when the body isn't introduced to a daily barrage of burgers, French-fries, candy bars, bon-bons and sodas. Limit the intake of these and other such items and you'll fare well. Side effects include increased energy, higher self-esteem, the need to shop for smaller clothes, and a general state of euphoria.

CLOSER:

Spare tire? Flabby arms? Fat thighs? Extra chins? *Exercise!*

A SEASIDE GIFT

Along a stony seaside path
A procession made its way,
Through trivial conversation
And the forenoon of the day,
To settle on a seaside cliff
Beneath a September sky;
To listen to a piper pipe
And family say good-bye.

Rivaled by sullen tears below,
The clouds held onto their rain.
The heather listened in the wind
While the ocean called his name.
And richer to have known the root
Of such a family tree,
They went with ashes in their hands
And gave their gift to the sea.

A THIRD PARTY

They live in a house
with four rooms they never use,
but in spite of their vacancy
each is decorated with
the best that money can buy.
The combined value of their vehicles
alone is more
than the GNP of some small nations.
Their wardrobe is a veritable
who's who of fashion designers.
A third party does their laundry.

They have a timeshare,
a condo at a ski resort,
and a membership at a country club.
They have an RV, a boat, a canoe,
two kayaks, a motorcycle, and two snowmobiles.
A third party walks their dog.

She has jewelry galore,
could feed a city block with the money
she spends on
makeup and perfume and facials and other
necessary
indulgences.
He has all the latest and greatest
gadgets, gizmos, thingamajigs and doohickeys.
He doesn't use any of them.
A third party does their landscaping.

They have six TV's.

Cable goes without saying.
They are on a first-name basis
at most of the high-end restaurants.
Their tickets for the symphony
and the pro games
are purchased for the season.
A third party does their grocery shopping.

They have a big fat mortgage.
They retain a lawyer.
An accountant does their taxes.
A third party cleans their house.

She works.
Him too.
She doesn't want to
but claims she has to.
He drops the kids off at daycare every morning.
She picks them up every evening.
A third party raises their children.

A WOMAN'S CHOICE

A tethered embryo
Yet to suckle at your teat
Of sustenance

Replete for daddy's
Satisfaction and breaths
Drawn through your teeth

At midnight in the bed
I will run to in thunder
And nightmare states

For comfort from ogres
Living under
A crib of straits

Until I multiply
In cellular division
To that exponent of power

That grasps and muses
And contemplates
The passing hour

That fuses me like solder
To the detriment of thought
And ultimate fate

This as all should be my lot
Though with uncertainty bound
And melancholy fraught

A chance to be of my own
Detached from which I am wound
Whether I am or I am not

AN ENEMY OUTRIGHT

be an enemy outright
don't call me friend
don't laugh and pretend
and then curse the night
watch you back
don't trust me
don't trust anyone
this advice I give you
because I hate the sport
we've made of hate
it will consume me
it will kill me
but it will kill you too

AN EXAMPLE OF INARGUABLE LOGIC

When questioning why I had to make my bed every morning, explaining that I was only going to mess it up again that night, my dad, in a moment of pure eloquence, looked at me and said:

"Why wipe your ass? You're only going to shit again."

I don't care if you're seven or seventy-seven, how can you argue with logic like that?

AND THE PEOPLE

meet and the people speak and the people laugh and the people cry and the people lie and the people pretend and the people are confused about not who but what they are and the people make up stories to fill the void of their expectations and the people feel failure and the people feel success and the people know hate and the people know jealousy and the people know selfishness and the people know vanity and the people see themselves age and the people wish they really knew the truth about heaven and the people fear death and the people know they will die and the people kill and the people work and the people know futility and the people dream and the people are reduced in the end like everything else to dust

ANTICONFESSIONAL

What I can't tell you about my family is the stuff you really want to know—the juicy stuff, the disreputable and base moments with all their sordid details. Like the time my father found my mother in bed with his brother, who years later announced at our family reunion that he was gay. I also can't tell you about the time my grandfather had to "go away for a little while," or because it was for racketeering. And I certainly can't share with you the details of my sister's expulsion from law school (it was only a small bag of marijuana). And although I'd rather like to tell you who slandered you, I'd better not—after all, we still don't have a lawyer in the family.

ARGUMENT

The protracted silence of our argument has lasted now a day,
And neither of us will use a word for what we have to say.
Instead we close a door a little harder than we should,
Or sigh a sigh when we know its meaning is understood.
Actions become our words, though none has a definition;
We know their meanings move us to our mutual submission;
To when the game is over and the rule of silence broken:
That reuniting moment when at last a word is spoken.

AS A MAN SO LEAVES HIS YOUTH

Suppose you took a walk
To accompany Autumn
On her meandering stroll
Through Summer's green

And suppose you asked her
For the secret of the touch
That turns all green to gold
And climes from warm to cold

And suppose she whispered
With hair-raising breath
That the secret of her season
Was in fact the touch of death

And suppose she reached for you
To impart her wisdom twice
But you withdrew your fellowship
To avoid that sacrifice

And suppose in turn she smiled
At the rejection of her truth
And left you to your ignorance
As a man so leaves his youth

POEM IN POEM

~~Suppose you took a walk~~
~~To accompany Autumn~~
~~On her meandering~~ stroll
Through Summer's green

And ~~suppose you asked her~~
~~For the secret of the~~ touch
~~That turns all green to gold~~
~~And climes from warm to cold~~

~~And suppose she whispered~~
~~With hair raising breath~~
~~That~~ the secret ~~of her season~~
~~Was in fact the touch of death~~

~~And suppose she reached for you~~
~~To impart her~~ wisdom ~~twice~~
~~But you withdrew your fellowship~~
~~To avoid that sacrifice~~

~~And suppose in turn she smiled~~
~~At the rejection~~ of ~~her truth~~
~~And left you to your ignorance~~
~~As a man so leaves his~~ youth

AS I WAS YOUNG

As I was young and fatherless
    And barefoot in my care;
While mother cried I knew not why
    But had the sense to dare—
When still my days came in like waves
    So soft upon the last;
The ebb to come decades away
    But closing on me fast—
Worry waited akimbo
    On the horizon for me;
Regret tapped a foot in time
    With Responsibility.
With ease I was a soldier
    Or a captain or a king—
In short I in a wink was all
    Without being a thing.
My diction failed in eloquence
    Yet held a certain charm;
An innocence preceding hate
    That caused no real harm.

Oh, days when I was young,
    With sweat of play upon my brow,
From whence has come this listlessness
    Attending to me now?
Where has flown my fancy,
    Upon which cloud does it reside?
And what of sweet simplicity
    Not long ago my guide?
The specter of mortality
    Is growing in my mind,

Growing out of dreams deferred
    And ambitions left behind.
Bring to me my innocence!
    Restore it in every part!
Return pure fascination
    To my mind and to my heart!
Alas, the sun is setting
    On the daytime of my heart;
And I at twilight regretting
    This end so near the start.

ASHES TO ASHES, DIAPERS TO DIAPERS

Life is full of loneliness and misery and suffering and unhappiness, and it's all over much too quickly.
—Woody Allen

From diapers to diapers we make our way through the forenoons, afternoons and evenings of our days. We end in very much the same way we begin: limp, weak, reliant, sleepy, drooling and shitting ourselves, calling those we love by the wrong names.... We begin with nothing to remember and end with nothing we can remember. I think the whole damned thing is just perfect!

AT HER OWN HAND

The question everybody asks is *why?*
But not I, I know exactly why.
No, my question is not why,
rather it is *for whom did you die?*

Your feigned anger, Lady Lazarus,
your contrived simulation of true hate,
was as distorted as your stretched reflection
on the convex side of the silver birth-spoon
clenched between your perfectly straight teeth.

Like some tenacious dog pulling on
the other end of a juicy bone,
you refused to relinquish your resentments,
until, ultimately, they relinquished you.

No, you were not angry, you sought pity,
attention, the sympathy of those too lazy
to look into the eye pits of an attention-starved
drama queen. You have seen your final curtain.

The show now over, I see the answer to my question:
For whom did you die?
In the ultimate act of selfishness,
you, at your own hand, died for yourself.

ATTITUDE PLATITUDE

I have a lousy attitude
today, it's like a bad back—
it won't let me get comfortable,
no matter how I stand or sit or lie.

Maybe I'm feeling sorry
for myself, as if I've got it bad.
Hell, I've got it made, and still
I could take it or leave it.

You know, if I could just get it,
perspective, that is, I'd be fine.
Someone else's misfortune
would make me feel better, I'm sure—
well, not better, but maybe a bit
guilty for having a bad attitude.

Then again, feeling guilty might
bring on an even worse attitude,
and that wouldn't be good—
you know, that whole insult-to-injury thing,
that digging-the-hole-deeper bit,
that mountain-out-of-a-molehill jazz.

You know what? Maybe I'll just try that
Mind-over-matter routine, or that
it's-only-what-you-make-it stuff...

Nah, I think I'll just stick with this whole
stewing-in-my-own-juices,
feeling-sorry-for-myself thingamajig.
Yeah, that's what I'll do.
That seems to be working.

AUTUMNAL REVELATION

I speed home,
leaves swirling
in golden eddies behind me,
stirring
the hearts of those
with not so brisk a pace.

BECAUSE

Because I arose before you
and saw the sunrise while you slept—

Because I sipped coffee in the dawn's silence
before the dew disappeared—

Because, on this particular morning,
a doe and her fawn walked through our garden
while I ate toast and watched them through
the kitchen window in reverence of their gentle way—

Because I want to share everything with you,
I will tell you none of this.

BETWEEN THE LINES

Like the fate of a two-legged table,
Whose top is heavy and base too narrow,
When one word fails it can topple a ton,
Proving that writing is but as stable
As the wind upon which sings the sparrow
Whose fragile song fades with each setting sun.
How can I say what none has been able?
The archer to split in half his arrow
So precisely that two are drawn from one?
It's the intimation in the fable
That puts the moral into our marrow
With more sense than if every word were spun.
    What's not said can say more than what's spoken:
    Words too many leave the meaning broken.

BEYOND ICE

It doesn't get any colder than ice,
my daughter says to me.
But she has much to learn about the cold,
about the unpleasant realities of temperature.
Mercury may sink deep, my dear,
deeper than the point that binds water to itself,
deeper on the scale than where the air freezes,
or deeper still, beyond the mark where stones split apart,
or where the rings of trees creak until they crack.
No, I explain, ice is just the beginning of cold.
It's the proverbial tip of the iceberg.
I was talking about his heart, dad.
I know, sweetheart. I know.

BIBLE SALES

Oh, you ragtag riffraff hoi polloi,
I'm your champion, your poster-boy—
Unkempt, disheveled, a general wreck,
A martyr willing to stick out his neck.
Love me or hate me, it's no matter,
The former always precedes the latter.

Now you've come to give up my ghost
And string me to your whipping post,
Because what's popular is so awhile
But rarely if ever comes back in style.
And though this will prove a fatal hook,
It'll surely help me sell my book!

BIRD FLU

My parakeet has the sniffles.
His head aches and he can't shake the chills
that cause his little wings to tremble but not flap.
He refuses the aspirin and hates the nasal spray,
and although his throat is sore, he rejects the lozenge
that would soothe the sting and restore his song.
He's weak and tired and I wonder how he has held
onto his perch for so long without falling off.
I want him to lie down and drink plenty of fluids,
but he just coughs and turns away from the thermometer,
deciding it's best to let these things run their course.
But he's just a parakeet, what does he know about sickness?

BODY LANGUAGE

Toe-to-toe because we can't see eye-to-eye,
Ready for a head-to-head in hand-to-hand,
We're neck-and-neck in this face-to-face,
Need a heart-to-heart before mouth-to-mouth.
Walk hand-in-hand or dance cheek-to-cheek,
Stand side-by side and shoulder-to-shoulder,
Not nose-to-nose or back-to-back—
Because I don't know what you're saying!

BUTTERFLY

Aflutter is the rainbow,
then still for me to count its colors
too great to list in this small space.
It lights upon a leaf
and makes it greener by its visit.
And I, distracted from the same duty
that calls again in the tomorrows
of a bare winter, lay down my hour
to behold a moment a-flood with life,
a-flood with puddles that shrink into ice,
a-flood with people who waste their lives.

BY SIGHT BUT NOT SOUND

Of all the senses one could lose,
Like the ability to smell a rose,
I think that losing the sense of sight
Is bigger than one million is to eight,
Though as for that a man gone deaf
Would say a tree without a leaf
Is like a heart without a love,
Or like a pool into which one dove
And found it empty but couldn't hear
The agony that few could bear,
But instead see only the awful wound
And not appreciate the sound
Of he who jumped to take the lead—
He who now would rather be dead.

CASTAWAYS

the face of a child
like stone
the downcast eyes
the slumping shoulders
the arms hanging in heavy flanks
the gravity of the downtrodden
the end achieved
the conclusion both giving and taking
and life itself a house of want
broken and vacant in a world
filled with inconsequential consequence
and intentional indifference—
we are the castaways of our own planet

COLLATERAL DAMAGE

the term defies sensibility
with its tidy little label for the gruesome reality
that millions have and will again be blown to pieces
in the misnomer name of progress

COLLISION

The wisdom of the bumper sticker,
The heartache in the song,
The NO-LEFT-TURN sign saying
What I just did was wrong.

COMING BACK AS A BUG

My Hindu friend tells me that,
unless I want to come back as a bug,
I'd better not kill the mosquito about to bite my arm.

Right, I say, and ready my hand for the swat.
I'm not joking, he warns, his look of concern genuine.
You can't be serious.
I'm very serious.

So, I should let the mosquito bite me?
Well, no, you should just shoo it away.
Just shoo it away?
Yes, just shoo it away.

I'm gonna pulverize the little sucker right now.
Okay, but just be ready to face the consequences.
What about West Nile virus and, say, malaria?
You should just shoo it away.

The telephone rings and my friend excuses himself.
Don't step on any bugs on the way in, I quip.
Very funny, he says.

I look down at the mosquito anchoring itself to my arm,
preparing its needle for the red withdrawal of my blood.

I wonder what it did in a past life to become a mosquito,
and then I decide that I don't really care
because the whole line of thinking is just ridiculous.
Smack!

I heard that, comes the faint voice from inside the house.
Shit! I think, I guess I'm coming back as a bug.

CORPUS CALLOSUM

the two of us are split
cleaved like an ass down the center
as if some mighty axe gashed apart
our dictionary of civility
now our mouths are tired
and we've nothing more to say
that won't be misconstrued
or lashed back upon us
in a flogging of absurd words
so we sit on curved couches
and wait for the mediator brain
to interpret what we mean
the invisible equator between
the northern and the southern
charges seventy an hour
to nod and say little
we push and pull simultaneously
against the resistance between us
the filter of arbitration tell us
we are two magnets with the same pole
we attract the same and repel the same
we are better off apart

DEATH AT SEA

The sea swells.
The horizon shrinks.
The sun sets sooner.
And I, a landsman lost,
float under the sagging canvas
of a powerless schooner.
My craft, between salt and stars,
warbles out the lament of its age
in notes only the sea understands
upon this, my final stage.

DEATH IN THE DESERT

A pinion in the sun,
A deception in the sand,
A canteen's comfort done:
A meal close at hand.

DÉJÀ VU TWO

Remember the past,
The before,
The ago,
And know
The ago past before,
Remember?

DISTRACTED BY A PRETTY WAITRESS

I've taken too big a sip of coffee—
more a swig than a sip, really—
and learned too late its scalding temperature.
At thirty-seven and thousands of cups of coffee,
you'd think I'd know the caution required
to avoid a burned mouth and the embarrassment
of spitting coffee back into a cup
in front of all these patrons
and one very, very pretty waitress.

DONE

You stared at me, your mind drifting away,
drifting right through the sight of me as I spoke.
Your inner eye focused on the memory of him.
I but a boring lecturer recounting his day,
a nameless invitation for you to share yours.
But I had finished and now waited in silence
for you to say something, anything at all.
But you just stood there, looking at me,
looking right through me, still nodding your head.
Hello, I said, *hello. Are you listening to me?*
I'm sorry, what were you saying?

DRIVING WITH THE MAGIC MAN

Magic seemed my father's specialty,
and he was quite the entertainer
to his audience of three in the back seat.
My sisters and I thought it a miracle
how he, with his hands clasped behind his head,
could steer our car down the highway.
And just how did he know exactly when
the light was going to turn green?
Counting the seconds down...3-2-1-go!

Later we learned about the knee.
Later we learned to watch the light of the cross street.
Later, much later, we learned he really did know magic.

DUTY

A flicker scatters a mist.
A bird sings me out of sleep.
A cheek ever gently kissed—
Oh, the promises I keep!

ECONOMICS 101: THE NEED TO EAT, AKA THE REASON DESIGNER SHIRTS EXIST

It all starts with the need to eat.
This is the cornerstone of economics.
The rest is mere contrivance and fluff.

The whole thing goes something like this:

We are born.
We get hungry.
We need food.
We need to eat.

So we hawk designer shirts at stores in malls owned by others who need to eat.

To get to the shirts, we drive cars made by folks who need to eat, on roads paved by others who are very hungry and need to eat.

We pump gas refined by people who are famished and need to eat into tanks at stations run in shifts by peckish attendants who need to eat.

And so it goes, and so it goes, every product made and sold the world over by a hungry lot of beings is done so because we need to eat.

At home in our pajamas, at a drive-thru in our jeans, at a restaurant in a designer shirt—no matter where or what we wear—we need to eat.

EGOISTS

I loathe the egotistical
With all their self-import,
The highbrow and the whimsical,
The snobby egghead sort.

As one not near so laughable
Or irksome like a flea,
I find myself quite affable
And prefer to speak of me!

ET TU

To refer to nature as anything but ourselves
is to refer to the oceans as anything but water:
Split an atom with a hippopotamus
and still we are the same.

Nature heralds nothing; we herald ourselves.

EXORCISING THE PAST

Too many people live in the past,
in their childhoods, in bad relationships,
or in good relationships no longer theirs....

I think we could all use annual exorcisms—
I'd even go so far as daily.
Just before bedtime would be good—
you know, so that you could get a good night's sleep.
The bathroom would be a good spot.
After all, that's where most purging takes place.
You could stand over the sink,
look into the mirror at your reflection,
and tell the demons of the day hasta la vista.
Let's start tonight, okay?

EZRA'S ACROSTIC

Lunacy
Often
Obscures
Meaningful
Insight,
Sadly:

When
Ezra
Sang
The Cantos
Of
Nihilism.

FAMILY REUNION

Why do we do this, this periodic get-together,
this day of hotdogs balanced on paper plates
designed to bend under the weight of a single pretzel?
'Hello, I've-never-seen-you-before, how are *you* doing?'
'You can remember when I was *how* tall? That's amazing!'

(Have we met?)

Okay, this getting old is getting old.
I should've brought more beer, I think
as I plan my escape from a picnic table
and a woman who calls herself my auntie
but is really just someone's friend.
'I'm an astronaut.' 'Of course!' she says.
'Alrighty then...gotta go, got a big launch tomorrow.
Nice seeing you again for the first time.'
'You too!'

(Yeah, right.)

But now an elderly woman with a mustache is trying to kiss
   me,
and a guy with a tattoo on each forearm is proving that his grip
   is stronger than mine,
and a little brat tugging on my pant leg is saying *mister, mister,*
   mister....
I feel like I'm at a carnival or a circus or something.
And then my cellphone doesn't ring, but I answer it, anyway.
'Hello. What's wrong? Really? I'll be right there.'
'Leavin' so soon?'
'Sorry, gotta go, my daughter is sick.'

'Theresa's sick? Hey, Marty, Theresa's sick.'
'No, not Theresa. Who's Theresa? Theresa's not sick. Julia's sick.'
'What! Julia's sick? Jesus! Harold, Julia's sick.'
'Theresa's sick?'
'Yeah, and Julia, too!'
'Something must be goin' around, eh?'

'Yes, something *is* going around.
In fact I'm feeling quite sick myself.
I'd better be going. Hope to see you next year. B-bye.'

FATHER TIME

(I've seen him on occasion
Lift his eyes and sigh,
Dizzy from the round and round
Of watching days go by.)

In retrospect at times it seems
I've lived a year in every day;
Still others when forever passed
More quickly than a wink away.

Not a nap, a stretch, or a yawn
From hoot of owl to shrill of cock—
A quirky one, that Father Time,
To never slow or stop his clock.

Oh, he keeps a perfect ledger
Under an ever-watchful eye,
Subtracting from infinity
All of the moments flying by.

True that I'll not live forever
Or have even a tick to keep—
But unlike you, Old Father Time,
At least I get to sleep!

FEAR

A child isn't born afraid of the dark.
The dog afraid of thunder
Cowers under its master's hand.

FEAST OR FAMINE

While my elder neighbor filled his pantry
With food in case of famine, and drink in case of drought,
I emptied mine of any hint of preparation,
Deciding instead to indulge to the fullest in the present.
He just watched and waited, shaking his head in disgust.

Well, the famine never came. The drought never arrived.
And now his stockpile is rotten and must be thrown away.
I just watch and shake my head in pity at his loss.

But he is not deterred; I know he wants to win our little war.
So, to prove his point, he is back at it, filling again his bins and
   shelves
With the ounces his father said would save him pounds.
I just smile and nod in silent recognition, not of his prudence,
But of that little piece inside me that knows I got lucky.

Perhaps one day I will concede the fight,
Revealing to him a secret hoard he did not know I had,
Or perhaps on the day I stand hungry at his door,
Waiting with hope to see if he is willing to share.

FIFTEEN EPIGRAMS FOR NO ONE IN PARTICULAR

I

The grass has taught me
What 10,000 generations of men could not:
It will outlast our flag too.

II

Raise your sticks all you want:
The tides of time erase
All lines drawn in the sand.

III

The moon is an old soul:
Its tranquil sea is filled with 10,000 tides
Of earthbound pensive eyes.

IV

The stone-still pond defies the wind,
Not out of spite or jealousy,
But because it is frozen.

V

The rain falls when it wants to:
Clouds may have silver linings,
But even the smoothest plank is filled with splinters.

VI

The potter's hands have fumbled the clay.
His image lies cracked and broken:
His creation ready for the eternal kiln.

VII

The puppeteer has tangled his strings
Deciding between right and wrong.
The fly in the web is afraid of God.

VIII

History remembers not good but evil.
Hearts are very much the same way—
Dogs, too.

IX

The hen's forked tongue is swollen.
She makes up lies for all she is not
And befriends those she cannot trust.

X

Can a question teach?
Should I hope to become a bud on the tree
Whose roots will cleave my coffin?

XI

The shark that ate the tourist is asleep.
It does not know that it has ruined a vacation,
Nor does it care.

XII

The principal difference
Between man and beast is simple:
Man knows he will die.

XIII

Justice, when a contrivance of expectation,
Is a false conception fostered by fools.
Our only just due is death.

XIV

Why look for mercy on the wind
When a sheep sinks its fangs to your bone?
Neither pity nor punishment can undo the done.
A stream cannot flow backwards into rain.

XV

I hope to live a life of retrospect.
May my days never be forecast.
May my nights be unknown until they happen.
I just want now. May I just have now.

FIST

"Don't you tell anyone!"
You said, shaking your fist
about an inch from my nose.
"If you tell anyone, anyone at all,
I'll knock your head off!"

And then, as if to punctuate your threat,
you spat in my face.

I can still smell the spit.

You were early thirties.
I was seven.
Needles to say, I didn't tell anyone.
Not a soul.
Until now.

When you are a young boy
and a grown man forces himself upon you;
when you have barely learned how to spell
let alone understand the meaning of a word like sodomy,
you are left with a lifetime of scars and questions.

The physical pain is one thing—
That goes away—
But frustration wrought by helplessness
has a permanence amplified by maturity.

Anyway, I could go on and on, but I won't.
I just know that tonight,
while rocking my newborn baby girl to sleep,
I thought that if you were here
I might show you a fist or two of my own.

FLUX

The ebb and flow, the wax and wane, the flux of everything.
An echo. An orbit. A birth. A season.
Distance grows and shrinks simultaneously,
As a yoyo's string uncoils to recoil:
Hand to floor, floor to hand, hand to floor.
The point to which one travels to the point from which one
 came.
And in the middle, a fulcrum, a near static point
Upon which teeters the infinitesimal possibility of equality.

FOUR, NOT FIVE

Staring through inoperable windows tinted a slight shade of black, I imagine that the stagnant air not fully exhaled from my lungs is like the coffee made at noon now thickening in its pot.

The rows upon rows of perfectly spaced fluorescent lights seem to me an upside-down Arlington and my ultimate fate, like the paperclip I am bending into the shape of a cross.

Now contemplating the fireable offense of destruction of company property, I bend another into a tight helix and throw it into a wastebasket filled with crumpled memoranda of very little significance.

It is an art to appear busy, and it takes more work than work to hide the tangible unrest shadowing the sunshine that waits for me, just on the other side of the black-shaded, inoperable windows.

FREE FALLING

You're climbing with friends in Arizona.
You're not sure, but it looks like the Grand Canyon.
You're not a climber,
but to keep things moving you decide the gear is borrowed.
The weather is perfect, except the sky's a strange green color.
You've never been to Arizona.

You're at about a thousand feet when—
all of a sudden—your line snaps
and you're in freefall, face-up,
looking back at your friends
with their hands outstretched towards you.
You reach back but now you can't even see their hands,
let alone the look in their eyes or the astonishment on their
    faces.
That's when you remember you're afraid of heights.
This isn't so bad, though, you think,
it's almost calm, almost relaxing.
The rush of air is nice,
your clothes and hair flapping before you,
the only sound, save the beating of your heart,
which seems much louder than it should be.
It's almost soothing, almost perfect.
Almost, but not quite.

And now you've managed to turn over in the air,
facedown, with the canyon floor rushing to meet you,
everything now much louder than before.
But now it's difficult to see
because your eyes have teared up and everything's blurry.
You know the canyon floor is just a second away,

not because you can see it but because you can sense it.

And then, just as you feel the ground touching
the outermost layer of your clothes,
there's a snap in your back, a sudden jerk in your neck,
and you're jolted upright in your bed,
startled to see the sun staring in at you,
his eyes barely above the windowsill.

FROM A BOAT UPON THE GREEN

From a boat upon the green and rolling fields of the sea,
the harvester of fish looks upon his children at play upon the shore.
What's lost in his age is drenched in duty and responsibility.
His impaired net cannot ensnare springtime or mermaids from the floor—
    neither youth nor age is deserved—
    but, alas, supper must be served.

FROM THE TOP

I want to pitch camp on your ego
drive tent stakes into your pride
start a fire on your alterside
to burn your high tree low
and rub my hands in the heat
of the blood in the pot I boil
to purify it for the soil
into which I will plant your feet
so that you can try it again

GIFTS FOR A MURDERER

Supreme Court will hear appeal today from triple-murderer who says lethal injection is unconstitutionally cruel
                —USA Today headline, 29 March 2004

Let me shoe you and clothe you.
Allow me to cut your hair.
I will buy all your groceries.
For work, have not a care.
Use all the hot water you would like.
I will pay for your lights and your heat.
Here is a room with a television.
Take the walls; they are yours to keep.
And here are books for you to study.
I will pay for your degree,
For of we two you are smarter:
You have left your worries to me.

GIVING UP

He sits with the best years for procreation behind him, diminished, reduced, but still capable. He thinks less often now about the girl of his dreams—her face, unlike his, ever smooth and supple, ever filled with possibility, with hope, with a chance for...whatever. He crosses his legs, ponders with indifference his waning virility, and decides, just as the feeblest are thinned from the herd, this is how things are supposed to be. This is nature's way. Besides, he thinks, the girl of his dreams is just that, a dream. Nothing is fixed; even memories fall languid. He rises to go. He is dead in a year.

HAIKU SUNSET

The egg dribbles its
Yolk over the horizon—
Cock-a-doodle-doo!

HAPPINESS

larva's not a pretty thing
though I would eat it
if I were starving
whole spoonfuls of it
like cottage cheese
with my nose pinched shut
and my eyes squinched up
because smell invites
tastes that don't please
and sight's tied to my gut
but with my eyes shut I know
that the unsightly sustenance
would flow to where it turned
to butterflies in my stomach
and my hunger would be satisfied
with my other senses pacified

HE WHO ADMITS WHEN HE IS WRONG IS WISE

He who admits when he is wrong is wise:
There is a lesson in every mistake.
Do not choose blame when guilt lowers your eyes.

Denial, that shield of unwieldy size,
Is pierced by truth like the bite of a snake.
He who admits when he is wrong is wise.

Blame is a game in which there is no prize,
Only the loss of one's pride is at stake.
Do not choose blame when guilt lowers your eyes.

Pointed fingers stir the pool of demise
And ripple one's reflection in their wake.
He who admits when he is wrong is wise.

How ill to do and then plot and devise
When caught with what you claim you did not take.
Do not choose blame when guilt lowers your eyes.

Turn your finger upon yourself and rise
A man willing to admit his mistake.
He who admits when he is wrong is wise.
Do not choose blame when guilt lowers your eyes.

HIGGLEDY-PIGGLEDY

Higgledy-piggledy
Red wine and chivalry
Might get you in the door—
But when tossing and turning
With itching and burning,
My man, the woman's a ....

HOW A BOY BECAME A POET

Drinking from a chamber pot
At four my grandmum found me—
Lemonade, I thought, perhaps,
But the taste did quite astound me.

At five I knew the dog would bite
Like all the other bitches—
Yet I yanked her tail and heard her wail
When they took me away for stitches.

At six they warned the pot was hot
When I reached for its tempting handle—
The same they said when I scalded my head
As the flame of last week's candle.

Seven I thought a mite tender age
To learn I could not fly—
But the kite on my back did not stop the crack
Of gravity's hello or good-bye.

At eight I donned my father's skis
And headed down the mount—
Then awoke to laughter several days after
With breaks too many to count.

At nine the wire called me,
So I answered it almost mocking—
But the advice my father gave me
Proved to be quite shocking.

At ten again high in a tree,

With a friend below supporting me—
I reached for a branch and near wet my pants
When it snapped like something inside me.

Would eleven come with much the same,
Then twelve and thirteen, too—
Till I just couldn't stand it and let loose the bandit
That fractured my attitude?

No, I said with a gash in my head
And a branch about to ensue—
I am done with fun that burns like the sun
And renders me black-and-blue.

I sprang to my feet and exclaimed in retreat
That I would never go back again—
Then stole to my room not a moment too soon
And took up a paper and pen.

I wrote of burns and breaks, cuts and scrapes,
But broke neither a bone nor a dare—
I told of my daring in a new bearing
That harmed neither my hide nor my hair.

And this is how I tell you now
Of a boy who once didn't know it—
But led astray too far one day
Found in himself a poet.

I AM NOT THE POET

I am not the poet naming
The flowers of his garden—
Chrysanthemum and lily,
Daffodil and daisy—
Using each in a string of strange
Metaphors nobody understands.

I am not the poet walking
Though some mystical forest,
Lost and not wanting
To find his way back home,
To where his wife of thirty years
Waits with a cup of chamomile tea.

I am not the poet sailing
Some distant tempestuous sea,
En route to or fleeing from
Some life event to which
He will succumb or endure,
Surrender or survive.

I am not the poet screaming
From between the bars of his
Impoverished and imprisoned language,
Which will never let him tell you
Exactly what it is
He really means or wants to say.

I BELIEVE

I believe a day is nothing more than a series of decisions.
I believe thoughts of the past can diminish the present.
I believe anxiety about the future can dispatch today.
I believe a search for happiness can create unhappiness.
I believe it is possible to have both faith and intellect.
I believe life should be lived as though it were ephemeral.
I believe man will destroy himself before he destroys the earth.
I believe there is no such thing as tomorrow.
I believe time is nothing more than distance.
I believe we struggle more than any other animal.
I believe nearly all our struggles are self-induced.
I believe we dilute our lives by believing in forever.
I believe religion is mankind's greatest bane.
I believe we outcast those we do not understand.
I believe that prejudice and hate are learned behaviors.
I believe ignorance is passed from generation to generation.
I believe man is his own worst enemy.
I believe we have laws because we have forgotten how to live.
I believe we punish our kind so that most will conform.
I believe most wars are fought over money in the name of religion.
I believe our separation from nature will be our demise.
I believe action is the catalyst to achievement.
I believe a man should never dismiss his own thoughts.
I believe blame prevents happiness and ruins lives.
I believe it is impossible to teach a man while he is talking.
I believe humans desperately need to believe in something.
I believe a man can convince himself of anything.
I believe no man can know the love of a mother.
I believe we are not greater than other animals.
I believe we are merely a rung on the ladder of evolution.

I believe no matter what we achieve or create it will not last.
I believe a man can learn more from a dog than a king.
I believe the prospect of everlasting life is a tasty placebo.
I believe nothing I believe should matter to you.
I believe life is beautiful.

"I'LL BE RIGHT BACK"

Why would there be a second thought?
He said he'd be right back.
Just a quick trip to the store for more of what it takes—
another gallon of milk, another loaf of bread.
But there she stood in the kitchen on the phone
in her disbelieving Sunday-same pajamas at noon.
There'd been an accident. It could be him.
But he had a soccer match later that day,
it couldn't be him.
For Christ's sake! The store was just five minutes away!
Could she come down to the hospital,
you know, to identify the body,
to make sure it was her John Doe
taken from the intersection of Hilltop and Spring?
She dialed his cell phone,
but the recording said the cellular user
had reached his destination.
The store was on the way to the hospital,
but that couldn't be his blue Chevy
turned upside down by the crumpled Lincoln.
The milk dripping through
the shattered windshield had to be somebody else's.
But there he lay, his identity confirmed in a single shriek.
And there, on his left wrist,
last year's anniversary gift ticking away—
its date correct, its movement precise,
its unflinching hands keeping perfect time
going around and around and around
like the wheels of an upturned Chevy.

I.R.S. AUDIT

I want to be adducted by aliens,
green ones with oversized eyes
and protruding antennae,
like the ones in cheesy sci-fi flicks.
I want to ride in their shiny saucer
to a distant planet in some far-flung galaxy
lying beyond the reach of our scopes,
where their leaders pace on roach-like legs
in eager anticipation of my arrival.
And I want them to talk about me—
right in front of me—
in a language I don't understand,
a language whose words sound to me,
I imagine, like my words sound to my dog.
And I want them to use gadgets unlike I've ever seen,
gizmos with buttons whose functions are a mystery.
But most of all I want them to take me home...
before they decide to cut me open
to find out what I'm made of.

IN PRAISE OF NUMBER ONE

I met a four one more than three
And twice as much as two,
And one was but a quarter of
That fourth one in the queue.

But then a five three more than two
And two more than the three
Outdid the four, one-upped the score
And made the one seem wee.

But half a dozen equals six
And six can hold a lot:
Have you three twos, six ones, two threes?
Then six is what you've got.

But seven is one more than six
And several more than four,
So even though six seems a lot
Seven is oddly more.

The next house on the number street
Is even number eight,
And you can move a four right in
With room enough for mate.

But neighbor to the eight is nine
And slightly bigger, too,
For nine can fit a one and six
With room left for a two.

One digit each has one through nine

But they're the last that do—
The number ten is bigger yet
And thus requires two.

And so it goes one more the next
And one more after that—
One more, one more, one more, one more,
One more than tit for tat.

But back at the beginning sits
The reason numbers mount—
It's that lowest of all digits
That makes the others count.

Without the one there is no two
Or three or four or five.
In fact without the one it's true
No number could survive.

So praise to you, sole number one,
The first of all the run—
Praise to you the only number
Without which there'd be none.

INERTIA

Like fortunes lost through pocket-holes
one penny at a time,
so too a life leaks out its toll
upon every hour's chime.

Like when the chains go slack
because you've swung too high,
so too a life keeps nothing back
while physics still apply.

FIRESIDE WINE

If I never love again
I will have loved but one
whose every touch upon me lit
more lovely than the sun.
And sure as flowers seek the warmth
relieved in light by drops of rain,
you are to me the fireside wine
that eases even my deepest pain.

JE NE SAIS QUOI NI QUAND

There is in life too little time
To swoon or court or woo,
Lest all life's importunity
Be false though purported true.

Of what great import we turn
Most matters trivial and bland!
Forsaking that which matters most—
This hour now at hand!

I know not what the future holds,
Nor when it arrives no more—
So be this moment upon me now
The last I'll ever ignore!

KINDNESS

Thank you for carrying my burden for so long.
I know that you are here to give it back.
But in a moment of pure selflessness
I have decided that you can keep it.
It's okay, there's no need to thank me.

LAST RIDE

His old soul heavy with seven years compressed into every one,
I lift my master of unconditional love and tireless devotion,
and carry him downstairs and outside to the awaiting car.

He has so often been the passenger seated at my side,
so often the listener I wanted, the companion I needed.
But today I lay him gently down on his favorite blanket,
wipe the tears from my eyes, and reluctantly pull the car into
    drive.

LATE DECEMBER DAYDREAM

the indistinguishable
        shadows
flitting across the walls
                like mice
startled on a granary floor

darting through intermittent
        slats at dusk
                in a dance of fire and ice
lay no knock upon my door

they are to me
        a kerchief on a wind
rippling over a fabric
                sea
upon the ship that took you away
        away
        away from me

LAWYERVILLE

The coffee's cold in Lawyerville—the soup, too. The restaurants have no toothpicks. Patrons have to pick with their fingers. If you have to go to the bathroom, you'd better go at home. There are no public restrooms. The *Wet Floor* signs are long gone. In Lawyerville, you can't buy a bicycle, a skateboard, or a pogo stick. Canoes, kayaks, skis and parachutes are strictly prohibited, as are high heels, slingshots and BB-guns. Cosmetics and all other chemical-containing products must be purchased with a permit, which is available through City Hall and printed on cloth, of course, to avoid the liability of paper cuts. For fear that a streetlamp may burn out and thereby create unsafe walking conditions and invite a lawsuit to be filed by the pedestrian who accidentally steps off a curb and causes bodily injury to himself, no one is allowed outside after sunset. Cars have been illegal since 1999 after an airbag saved a life but broke the driver's glasses, which resulted in the vehicle's manufacturer paying a court settlement of millions after it was determined that the driver had suffered mild psychological damage caused by the loss of the glasses, which evidently held significant sentimental value and were irreplaceable. Grocery purchases are allowed only after signing a release of liability designed to protect the seller from suits over choking, slipping, spilling, scalding, and other household mishaps that may arise when preparing or consuming groceries. Boating is out of the question. Swimming pools are long gone, their diving boards and slides with them. Airplanes are a relic of the past. Baseball, basketball, football, hockey, soccer, and all other sports involving more than one person and/or a foreign object are not allowed, including weightlifting, gymnastics, track and field, checkers, chess, and tiddlywinks. Dogs are illegal. Cats are okay if they've had their claws and teeth removed and if they receive regularly scheduled weekly shavings to reduce the potential of allergic reactions in unsuspecting houseguests. Houseguests are illegal unless pre-approved in writing by a committee that deems the houseguest to be of sound body and mind and who has no pending legal action against a third party. Parties are illegal, including birthday parties, which require burning candles atop a cake. Matches, lighters, candles and cakes are also illegal. Using the word illegal is illegal, as is burping, farting, or thinking. Welcome to Lawyerville!

LESSONS

Of all the lessons
my father tried to teach me
with the buckle-end of his belt,
there is only one I can remember...
okay, none.

LIES

The real history of consciousness starts with one's first lie.
—Joseph Brodsky

Innocence ends with language; the ability to tell a story; the power to construct a lie. And with it begins the painstaking and regrettable task of having to remember fact from fiction: a losing endeavor in which one must guard for the rest of his days against that inevitable moment of inattention when at last he stands exposed, saddled with the heavy deficit of deceit, naked and ashamed in the light of the truth.

LIVING IN THE PAST

Current events are highly overrated.
I prefer to live in the past. It's easier there.
Consequence is, well, inconsequential.
The bad is just as easy to take as the good.
And mistakes?—who cares! They don't even matter.
Besides, you already know what's going to happen.
That's the beauty of living in the past—
You can be a goddamned know-it-all
And *really* know it all!
How pleasurable and powerful to know with certainty
The events, the times, the places—every little detail!
The past is where it's at!
(Unless of course you want to live.)

LONGING

Yet another winter is upon me,
and yet again the sun-short days
spread out upon the lake
until every depth succumbs to ice.
And now the mirror will not ripple
but shatter into countless prisms
under the stiff weight of longing
for the coalescing touch of spring.
Oh, when are you coming home?

LOST SHEPHERDS

On occasion our father would send him
To round up the sheep grazing in the fields
We owned but could not see from our house.
The back pasture was a long walk for a boy
With an imagination as big as his.

Cresting that rise between duty and freedom
Revealed to him a boundless world in which
A boy could dream beyond his pillow,
Beyond his father's want and expectation,
Beyond his prescribed and inherited future.

This was his favorite chore, although unknown
To our father, with whom he learned never
To show emotion but mental indifference
For fear that he construe happiness for weakness
And send instead me to fetch the sheep.

And he did, of course, the day after he went
To punish him in the pasture for being gone so long,
But found instead his body beneath the field's only oak,
A good-bye note to me in his left hand;
His favorite pistol fallen from his right.

LOVE LETTER FROM A LAWYER

My dear, hereinafter you, may this letter serve as full disclosure of my love for you. Be advised, however, that the opinions expressed herein are those solely of the writer and may not be shared by others. This letter is not intended to serve as a guarantee of future love, which is subject to change without notice. Rather, insofar as the hitherto unexpressed love remains in full force and effect, it should be understood that, henceforth, until such time of revocation in writing of the aforementioned love, I love you. It should further be understood that, notwithstanding acts of war, whether declared or undeclared; felonious acts, including such misdemeanors considered violent or otherwise malicious in nature; lascivious, lewd, or generally unacceptable behavior, defined as any behavior that has or is likely to cause disapproval, dislike, discord or dismay; acts of indiscretion or infidelity, including implied infidelity, such as implicit unfaithfulness exhibited through an act of flirting with anyone other than he expressing his love herein; keeping an unkempt, disheveled, or generally undesirable or unclean appearance; excessive weight gain; strange fetishes, peccadilloes or other tics or desires that are either not liked or mutually shared; any marked negative change in disposition, attitude, outlook, demeanor or optimism; moral decline or loss of sound decision-making; taking up smoking, heavy drinking or any drug that is now or may become illegal, I intend to love you indefinitely. It should be understood, however, that *indefinitely* is a relative term and is therefore at the sole discretion and interpretation of the interpreter[†], a.k.a. me. Consequently, any aforementioned love, whether stated or implied, may be deemed null and void at an indeterminate date and will thereupon cease and desist, unless, of course, at the sole discretion of the undersigned, suitable reparation, consolation or groveling deems such love reinstated. In any such instance, however, any such reconstituted love will still be subject to the conditions disclosed herein. Other than previously described conditions set forth in this letter, my love for you is unconditional*.

The undersigned, as a duly authorized representative of his own feelings, and being of sound mind and body, hereby acknowledges and expresses the above-promulgated love for you (subject to the terms and conditions set forth herein and any other conditions which, from time to time, may arise).

Sincerely,

Yours**

† 1976, Supreme Court, Smith v Smith
*In accordance with open interpretation, *unconditional* may not necessarily mean *unconditional*
**Figuratively speaking

MARRIAGE

Marriage is as natural as a caged bird—
The notion of two together forever absurd—
'I do' the longest sentence ever heard.

MAYBE I COULD MAKE A MILLION

If I could throw a football with precision,
maybe I could make a million.
If I could find the cure for cancer,
maybe I could make a billion.
If I could find a replacement for oil,
maybe I could make a trillion.
If I could place a phone call to God,
maybe I could make a zillion.
Maybe I should just watch TV
or stack Z's by the jillions—
besides, I already have a job.

MERRIMENT IN THE DOSE
(THE ASSASINATION OF THE KING)

"Is there not then any care
Within a person anywhere;
Nor thought enough nor aim
To turn from selfish gain
And ease the wretched soul
Of he falling short of his goal?"

Asked the king of those beyond the moat;
His boot pressed upon the assassin's throat.

"I beg your pardon, sire,"
Came a voice among the shire,
"But there's no poison in that grail;
'Tis filled for you with birthday ale.
In fact I think if you look close
You'll find but merriment in the dose."

The king with hesitation put his finger in the brew,
Touched it to his tongue and tasted it was true.

"You must excuse my manner,"
Said the king in a halting stammer.
"I fear I am overly cautious,
To a point it makes me nauseous.
I thank you for the birthday beer,
And will drink it now without a fear."

With that the king toasted the shire, grail raised above his head;
Then took a bolt, grabbed his throat, gasped and fell stone dead.

The shire stood in stricken quiet,
The kind that comes before a riot.
"Wait! Wait! I swear 'tis only ale!"
Cried the townsman, his skin now pale.
"Look, I'll drink the rest and prove it true,
That this is but a harmless brew."

The shire looked on with an interest that needs no mention,
For not a soul breathed, so rapt was their attention.

Aghast they stood in disturbing dread
When the townsman gulped and too fell dead.
Dumbfounded and frightened their knees grew weak
From the evil there of which no one dare speak,
Save a serf who muttered now he'd been freed,
"Ah, yes, merriment in the dose indeed."

MISSING

In the paper there is a picture of a missing girl.
She has been missing for eight years.
I examine her face and think of her parents:
How once they must have laid the gentlest touch
Of their fingertips upon her newborn brow;
How they must have kissed her nose and delighted in her
    laughter;
How they must have dreamed for her a perfect future;
How now they must not be able to forget the past,
Even though, with each new night,
How their hope, like the light, must fade.

MISTAKE REALIZED AT EIGHTEEN

Our child, this isthmus between us,
whom we have loved more than each other,
is but a tender sinew to which our hearts are tied.
Our lives stand two shores connected through a great fog
by a bridge ready to fall into a sea of difference.

MY OWN RELIGION

Spare us the stained-glass language.
                              —Archie Bunker

Tired of the ceremonial?
All that pomp and circumstance?
(Stand-kneel-sit-pray…stand-kneel-sit-pray…)
And what about all those silly little rules?
(Not to mention your guilty conscience.)
Well, have I got a deal for you:
Kneel down to me!
That's right!
Turn your life, your control, and your mind over to me!
Give your loyalty, your chastity, your industry—
    but most of all—give your money to me!
I'm starting my own religion.
And best of all, there's no church!
You're going to love it!
I'll get back to you soon with some names.

NAMES

Who am I among some six billion names?
Some letters so arranged that when spoken
I hear recognized my outward token
To the world, the face my mirror proclaims?
What *is* in a name? Consonants and vowels,
Mere syllables interrupted by breath?
Or history, future, the here and now;
The knowledge of life, the question of death?
And what without a language or a tongue?
How, then, would I or anyone be known,
If never a name could be said or sung;
If never a mark could be writ or shown?
    How beautiful if not by names or charts
    But the measure of love within our hearts!

NEVER TEST THE DEPTH OF WATER WITH BOTH FEET

At the same time I was learning how to ride a bike,
Gary Wolf, a neighbor boy of the same age,
Stayed inside, even on the sunniest of days,
To practice the piano his mother had practiced.

While I scaled the countryside hills of Braintree,
Gary sat at home, squirming on his piano bench,
Scaling his arpeggios and daydreaming about hopscotch
And leapfrogging over a row of boys whose names he didn't know.

While I played hide-and-seek and ring-around-the-rosy,
Gary learned how to massage the ebony and ivory keys
That would never unlock the door to his prison.
(He must still hear them clanging from his warden-mother's chain.)

I always felt sorry for Gary, although I envied his talent.
He surprised us all when he agreed to meet us
Down at Coggeshall Pond on Saturday morning,
The day of his ninth birthday.

None of the other boys noticed when he didn't show;
He had never come before, and it was easy to forget him.
But I noticed, and I stayed long after the others had gone,
Stayed until I knew my mother would be looking for me.

I suppose that when he arrived he may have felt deserted,
Duped, the butt of a mean-spirited joke.
He may have even called out my name—the only one he knew—

And searched the edge of the surrounding woods for our hiding faces.

I like to think that he leapt from the banks of Coggeshall Pond
And let out a scream with a pitch no piano on earth could duplicate.
And while in the air for that brief moment before the water swallowed him
With an unexpected gulp, he lived a childhood in an instant.

When his mother saw the open window out of which he climbed,
And when she found the tape player looping the recording of yesterday's lesson,
She must have called out his name over and over again.
But Gary never answered; he had never been swimming before.

NOAH

Wisdom cometh from suffering.
                    —Aeschylus

I

They must have thought him crazy, the old codger
Warning them of the destruction by deluge to come—
Sure, Noah, why don't you have a little more wine
And leave some gopherwood for the rest of us.

But the one good man, blameless among those of his time,
Persisted through the scorn and bound plank to plank—
The Lord's direction—until at last she stood in dry dock,
That laughable vessel of refuge from divine retribution.

How foolish he must have sounded to the naysayers
When he explained that the sea would come to him;
That only he, his family, and two of every kind would survive;
That God had chosen *him* to carry on the lineage of man.

Okay, Noah. Whatever you say, big guy. Nice boat, though.
And then, of course, the real mockery must have begun,
Not when he corrected them and told them that it was an ark,
But when he began to fill it with dodos and pygmy mammoths.

And soon thereafter the mockery must have turned to anger,
What with all the stench of animal waste and babel of wildlife—
Would you keep those damned hyenas and monkeys quiet!
And for god's sake, would you please clean up that rhino dung!

But old Noah, steadfast in his six-hundredth year of life,

Skilled in carpentry and how to distinguish the gender of gnats,
Kept his promise and gathered them up, two by two—
That menagerie destined for a new beginning, a second genesis.

II

And then it happened. The sky thickened and the sun dimmed.
And Noah, hands to heaven, at last felt in his palms the drops
Of the storm that in comparison to others was as Cain to Abel—
A killer whose sacrifice was his own brethren.

There must have been at least a few villagers who recanted
When the waters rose to the level that set the ark afloat.
And how awful Noah must have felt watching them perish,
Each outstretched hand disappearing one by one below the
    surface.

Even the pleas of those in the tallest trees were silenced—
Even those who scaled the heights of Kilimanjaro and Everest.
As Noah warned, not a soul among man or beast survived
That brackish Pangaean sea that swallowed the world.

III

Most readers remember only the forty days and nights of rain,
Forgetting the miserable one hundred and eighty days that
    followed—
The days when the sun beat upon the water to return it to the
    sky
And restore the mountains and the plains and the valleys.

Those were the days he must have walked the plank of
    madness—

The days he resisted the temptation of the T-bone and the chop;
The hours he came close to silencing the woodpecker and
 cricket;
The times he chose not to give the lamb to the lion or the fly to
 the frog.

Those were the days he must have cursed that zoo of funk and
 filth
That rocked and creaked in the unrelenting heat,
Floating aimlessly over untold villages, each an Atlantis,
Each now as obsolete as the inconsistent cubit.

IV

But he made it. The water subsided and the rainbow faded.
And at long last the dove returned with the leaf in its beak.
It was over. The unheralded savior of the earth had endured
The wrath and divine chastisement of an angry God.

Old Noah, that man from whom we are all descended,
That outcast who wrestled with but kept his faith,
Retired with his wife to the hills of Ararat
And died wise at the ripe old age of nine hundred and fifty.

NOTHING MADE CAN LAST, NOTHING WROUGHT CAN STAY

The monuments we erect to ourselves
Rise up predestined to decay—
The mounting dust a portent on the shelves,
The moss and rust, the crack and fray—
Nothing made can last, nothing wrought can stay.

Ideas like walls eventually fall,
Beliefs and customs pass away—
Pages of law written as good for all
Yellow away like grass to hay—
Nothing made can last, nothing wrought can stay.

All roses fade, all skies turn gray,
All prayers resign to come what may—
From womb to tomb we make our way,
As darkness comes to dying day—
Nothing made can last, nothing wrought can stay.

NOW AS AGO

As faded as a winter rose
Upon whose stem mere remnants cling,
She rests, at last, in final pose,
The life once such a splendid thing.
Now with an ease like summer rain
Down avenues of light she glides
Into that place where candles wane
Like starlight on receding tides.

Now as ago her mind is clear,
Now again her pretty face beams,
Now sharp anew her eye and ear,
Now again her heart full of dreams.
Now her feet as light as a girl's,
Again roses bloom in her cheeks;
Her hair renewed to buoyant curls,
Again the dream every boy seeks.

Now faded as a winter rose
Upon whose stem mere remnants cling,
She rests, at last, in final pose,
The life once such a splendid thing.

ODYSSEY OF THE ANT

The ant on the opened atlas on my roll-top desk
Makes fast work of Borneo,
Malaysia, Singapore, Indonesia,
And then steps off Jakarta onto the Indian Ocean.

No one living on the northwest coast of Australia
Need worry about the sea rising
Or beach erosion caused by a tsunami.
The ant is not concerned by or is unaware of
The depth of the Java Trench.

Within seconds it has navigated its way
South of Madagascar to Prince Edward Island,
And then east to Tasmania and New Zealand,
Pausing in Wellington before embarking
North for the Tropic of Capricorn.

Straddling the Solomon Islands,
It proves Micronesia a fitting name
Before sailing the mighty but miniature Pacific
North to Tokyo and the Sea of Japan.

Now, with a twist of its beaded body,
It unites North and South Korea,
And in a turn is on Mainland China,
Then meandering through Mongolia,
Unaffected by the desolate expanse of the Gobi.

Scaling the Himalayas with unprecedented ease,
And without leaving a flag for the next to conquer its height,
It's off to India, Pakistan, and the Caspian Sea,

Then backtracking briefly to Kazakhstan
Before passing through Syria and into Turkey.

I marvel at the stamina and design of its cabochon body,
Which now covers the name of a city half the size of Romania,
Home, I'm sure, to thousands who've never left their country
Or seen the likes of a four-hundred-mile-long ant.

Now in Greece, it turns south to the Mediterranean,
Pausing in Libya to mark the Tropic of Cancer,
Swiveling its head from east to west,
Noting the flattened Andes, the Not-So-Great Wall of China,
The miniature Sphinx, and the laughable Pyramids of Giza.

From hemisphere to hemisphere, I watch the global explorer
Make quick work of each of our seven,
And admire how, without finding so much as a crumb or a grain of sugar,
It leaves our world behind to embark on a much more difficult journey:
The far larger realm of an antique roll-top desk
Sitting in a room in a modest house in a small town
On the third largest continent on the third planet from the closest star.

OF ALL THE POEMS I HAVE WRITTEN, THIS IS PERHAPS THE ONE WITH THE LONGEST TITLE

Do not say a little in many words but a great deal in a few.
—Pythagoras

The poem itself, however, will not be long,
I promise you that.
In fact, let me say just this:
If brevity is the soul of wit,
It too is the soul of good poetry.

OF COMPLICATIONS FROM A FALL

Falling is rarely if ever complicated.
In fact, it's quite easy:
A slip here, a misstep there
And you're lying prone or supine
In a matter of a second.

It's what follows that's complicated:
The getting up,
The getting on.
Some people never do.

OH, THE BOOKS I OWN BUT HAVEN'T READ

Oh, the books I own but haven't read...
they, donned in their dusty jackets,
in disappointment, shake their heads
at me and mutter their tisk-tisk-tisk.

The mark of an amateur, they say,
to write more than he reads. I agree
but close my ears to their satirical
epithets and keep poking at the keys.

But they've joined their consonants
and vowels in an unbroken blurb,
weakened only by the occasional
ellipsis or extra extra adverb,

and they say intention without effort
will keep my dreams from fruition,
and is like the would-be scholar
off to college without his tuition.

I know. I know. I know. You're right.
I should put away my poetry for the night,
take one of you from the shelves, dust you off,
sit back, and listen to your alphabet—a to zed!

Alright. Yes. Okay. Uh-huh. Yep. I will.
Just give me a few more minutes to thread
the...last...couple...of...lines...into...this...poem....
Okay, I'm ready. Oh, damn! It's time for bed!
Oh, the books I own but haven't read...

ON WHAT'S ABOUT TO HAPPEN NEXT

The guy in the movie is about to make a big mistake, you think, but then you remember that he wasn't privy to the director's sneak-peek of the guy with the gun on the other side of the door. And while you appreciate the suspense, you can't help but feel that the director has cheated you out of the surprise. That's when you remember that the two guys in the movie won't be surprised, either. After all, they're actors, they read the script and know that at any moment the door will be kicked in and they'll start shooting at each other. They even know who will live and who will die. What really stinks, though, is that now you don't care what happens next, or how the movie ends. In fact, if you hadn't spent half your paycheck on popcorn and soda, you'd get up and walk right out of the theater, right out into the real world where you have no idea what will happen next, no idea what's waiting on the other side of the door—and that, you think, is very, very exciting.

ORDER
(written after reading *Removal*, an essay by E. B. White)

Order amid disorder or disorder amid order?
The rug I realign with the floor seams several times a day,
The cockeyed picture I straighten,
(Lest its watercolors spill out of its frame?):
Is mere symmetry my satisfaction?
And outside the grass grows every which way,
Stars are sprinkled haphazardly across the sky,
Branches grow out of branches at aimless angles,
Not one of which has the same knobs, bends, or girth—
Their leaves all irregular and disjointed.
And then, of course, there's the whole matter of snowflakes.
Perhaps next time I see my rug askew I'll leave it that way.
Perhaps I should just enjoy the painting.
Perhaps there is no order as perfect as disorder.

PEACHY

A wild dog—any one—licks its wounds,
Sure not to let a drop of its blood
Go to feed anything but itself.
In a prison—pick one—a man is shanked,
Forced to submit to sodomy,
And left in a heap on a concrete floor.
In a ghetto—that one'll do—someone's son
Is shot in the head and left for dead,
A rock the size of a pea in his pocket.
In a hammock under a tepid sun,
A man—pick me—bites into a peach,
Licks the juice before it falls from the fuzz,
Swallows the pit, and tries hard to fall asleep.

PEARLS BEFORE SWINE

We give value to the pearl,
That miraculous gem of the sea,
And therefore pry from unwilling jaws
That avoidance of penury:
The mollusk's immaculate creation,
Fashioned in matchless craft,
Which we, to embellish our worth,
Plunder in mindless graft.

'Tis true of all we assign a price,
Be it a pearl or an automobile,
Something is made a sacrifice
To gain that with human appeal—
Though pearls make us no richer
Than when we were conceived;
Rather, we grow impoverished
By the value we perceive.

PENCILS, PENS, PAPER

Asked to write a poem for friends
On the occasion of their wedding,
And considering the honor their gift to me,
I make my way downstairs and into my study
Where the implements of my craft wait
Ever ready to carry out the will of my hand,
Like they have so many times before.

Across my desk I see the familiar No. 2 pencils
Dressed in their predictable school-bus yellow.
Stiffened like a bouquet with rigor mortis,
They are content to lean against the mouth
Of the mason jar in which they stand,
Propped against its singular glass lip,
Which has not once said hello or struck up a conversation.

Incapable of uttering a single word, a single sound,
They have no power to scratch out a sentiment,
No muscle to stand on end and draft themselves a sonnet
Or even scrawl a forgettable haiku.
They cannot wield themselves across a page,
Speak of love or whisper a secret,
Tell you how they are doing or how their day was.

Without my hand, without my voice
They are mere wood and carbon, inanimate,
Static, mere potential without power,
As useless as a candle without a wick,
A wick without a flame.
Or perhaps they are more like an emotion never expressed,
A feeling never shared, a story never told.

Contemplating, my eyes fall upon two pens
Lying dormant beneath the pencils.
Though gilded and inscribed, they are no better.
They have no message of love
Coursing through their slender blue veins.
Like the pencils, their might is in my hands,
Their voice is in my lungs, their message is on my lips.

I lean back into the cool embrace of my writing chair,
The ceiling widening into a canvas for my daydreams.
How unfortunate, I think, to have only potential,
Only the prospect of what might have been
If only they had the power to express themselves.
But, with neither a pulse nor a will to share,
They are as empty as this ceiling, as blank as this page.

Slowly my eyes return to focus,
The intricate pattern of the ceiling gaining clarity,
My mind returning to the task before me:
A poem for friends on the occasion of their wedding.
The pencils stand ready to be plucked.
The pens ready for the final draft.
The paper ready for the poem to begin.

PERSPECTIVE

Is it human nature to look back
into the bowl at what just came out of us?—
the shape of shit, of what we ate yesterday
for lunch or dinner, the food we took care
to prepare with just the right mix of spices,
with or without a dollop of mayonnaise or tartar
sauce for our fish, our beef, our chicken?
And don't we all have to look at the paper
to know whether or not we need to wipe again?
You must know that Hitler on occasion had the runs.
Rest assured that Saddam's hand *has* slipped.
Know that the Queen of England, with one of her
royal gowns pulled up past her lily-white fanny,
has squeezed out breakfast upon her second throne.
Ahhh!—the emancipation of constipation—ahhh!—
perspective, perspective, perspective.

PI

Pick a number, A or B: math is not my forte. Still it is interesting to contemplate the imperfect math of the imperfect circle: how nothing has a precision so definitive we can call it exact. So I align a crude ruler across a diameter that's not quite in the middle of the circle whose circumference lies in the magical Pi. This, I think, is the first faulty factor in my equation. Still, I proceed to apply the incomputable ratio to my rough estimation, but now I must decide if 3.14 is sufficient, or if I should carry out the digits a few billion decimal places to make this calculation of great approximation a bit more accurate. Finally, I conclude that it is best to unfold the circle, stretch it into the straightest line I can, and lay it against the inconsistent inches of my imperfect measure. That is good. That, I decide, is close enough.

POET'S BLOCK

There is a poem I should have written,
But it was stolen from under my nose
And given to the one with whom I'm smitten—
Look! She walks with him, giggling as she goes.

To see taken the girl who should be mine—
Oh, 'tis enough to set me in a rage!
Muse, awaken! You leave my heart to pine—
For he has her, and I an empty page.

PORK CHOPS

she says I'm lazy
says I don't contribute
enough around the house
so I point to the floor
and remind her that I laid it
(four years ago, but I laid it)
I point to the wall
and remind her that I painted it
(two years ago, but I painted it)
she just stands there
shaking her head
a basketful of laundry
resting on her hip
she calls me little prince
it's your fault, I say
you made me this way
you've spoiled me
she's not buying it
and neither am I
you're just plain lazy, period
what do you want me to do
nothing, she says, nothing at all
I'll do the laundry
no, you'll screw it up
then what, what should I do
nothing, just watch the game
she walks away, still shaking her head
halfway down the hallway
I ask her, half-joking, what's for dinner
pork chops, she says, your favorite
I go back to the game
I'll do something tomorrow
after tomorrow's game

PREPOSITIONS ARE WORDS
YOU SHOULDN'T END SENTENCES WITH

My seventh grade English teacher taught me that
You shouldn't end sentences with prepositions.

He said that prepositions were words
You shouldn't end sentences with.

I mean prepositions are words with which
You shouldn't end sentences.

If the last word is a preposition,
You shouldn't end—

End with a preposition, at least
You shouldn't.

You shouldn't
End with a preposition, at least

You shouldn't end
If the last word is a preposition.

You shouldn't end sentences—
I mean prepositions are words with which

You shouldn't end sentences with.
He said that prepositions were words.

You shouldn't end sentences with prepositions.
My seventh grade English teacher taught me that.

RACCOON

I remember stories
my father told me about lame horses
put out of their misery by sensitive cowboys,
cowboys who wrestled
with the strange duality of giving while taking.

It was about the suffering.
It was about the inability to stop it,
the inability to cure it.
It was about humanity, mercy,
and doing the right thing.

I am not a cowboy.
I have never owned a horse or carried a pistol,
and I do not know the best way to stop the suffering
of an injured animal.

But driving home tonight I found my turn,
my chance at this awkward compassion,
my chance to join the solemn ranks
of those who have faced this decision,
this dilemma.

Suffering is not easy,
even, and maybe especially,
when it is not your own.
Suffering is not easy,
even after it is ended.

RAIL-SPLITTER

You said the train had jumped its tracks because it was tired of its destination, tired of the iron confinement of the rails, the raised ruts, the predictable landscape, the known turn, the upcoming climb, the ensuing descent. I said it was because the engineer was going too fast. You nodded, said humph, and left for work again.

READING THE DEAD POETS

The bards of yesteryear repose in muteness,
Dumb to their new critics' lack of astuteness.
Victims they lie of re-evaluation,
Buried anew by misinterpretation—
"This, I believe, is what he meant when he said..."
Indeed there are times when you're better off dead.

REARVIEW NAP

my daughter's cry is on the edge of shrill—
the awkward cry, I guess, of an owl kept up
all day like a melody of disuse
from my baby grand: my out-of-tune piano

the song of the wanted or unwanted
a wordless tirade
a discourse of dissatisfaction
and in a mile
silence

RICHARD CORY'S BROTHER

When Richard Cory's brother went down town,
    We people on the pavement knew his name:
He, too, a gentleman from sole to crown,
    Although balding and with one foot gone lame.

And he was always first to lend a hand,
    And sincere if ever he said sorry;
He was a gentleman whose life was grand,
    'Though he had every financial worry.

Oh, he was poor—yes, poorer than a mouse—
    But still he kept his threadbare clothing clean,
And a pride apparent in self and house
    Shinned as a beacon unlike we had seen.

So on we worked 'side him of whom we said
    'Twas unfair to compare to another,
And not surprised the day the paper read:
    Richard Cory, survived by his brother.

RUSH-HOUR DREAMS

to home
on the highway

people jockeying
for my way

thoughts drifting...
car, too

rush-hour dreams
of you

SAVE THAT BEAST CALLED MAN

Not a single squirrel sings in praise
Nor a fox bestow an accolade
Upon the clouds or rocks or rivers;

No spiders spin awards of merit
For things their egg-sacks shall inherit
From webs spun out of silken quivers;

Bears never make their achievements known
Or memorialize their names in stone
For the rest of their kind to covet;

The eagle's only prize is its prey,
The food it has no choice but to slay
Without conscience to hate or love it;

Whales never give themselves citations
Marking the stature of their stations
Or honoring their colossal span;

Not a beast heralds, lauds or praises
Itself, its kind, or those it raises—
No beast at all save that beast called man.

SCHOOL OF HARD KNOCKS

People ask me
after reading my poems—
Where'd you get your degree?
What school did you graduate from?
I answer them by saying *SOHK*.
Some give an affirmative nod,
not willing to admit they've never heard of it.
But most ask—
SOHK? Where's that?
Oh, they have campuses everywhere, I say.
Really? I've never heard of it.
Humph?

SEA-WINE SESTINA

Fashion for me a garden from this road,
Turn its pavement to a bed of flowers
Too beautiful to pluck or to trample;
Then make for me a blanket from the sea,
Of blue coral and white shells and green reeds
Sewn together with dune grass and feathers.

Make a pillow from hummingbird feathers
That have fallen along my garden road,
And place it for me on a bed of reeds
To rival my blanket and my flowers;
Then fetch me up the currents of the sea,
And bring a vintage for them to trample.

Then shut me away from days that trample
Dreams under the weight of rain-soaked feathers,
And let me consume the wine of the sea;
Let me sail on its boundless liquid road
In a craft made of my garden's flowers
And the wind-filled sail of my blanket's reeds.

Listen to the orchestra of the reeds!
Listen to the song of waves that trample
Shores in search of sun to feed the flowers
With sea-wine shaken from fallen feathers!
There is no agenda along that road
That sings to me with the voice of the sea!

If I could be as carefree as the sea!
If motives were mere whispers in the reeds!
Then there would be an end to this road

Upon which for gain I toil and trample.
Could my burdens turn as light as feathers,
And my hope as fresh as morning flowers?

Is it too much to have hope like flowers,
Or to become as carefree as the sea,
Or have burdens be as light as feathers,
And motives turning to whispering reeds?
If yes then let me forever trample
A vintage for those who travel this road;

Then give entrance to this road of flowers,
And trample a path of hope to the sea,
Where motives are reeds and burdens feathers.

SERENDIPITY

It came to me at last—
my childhood wish—
my longing and my aim—
it came to me a herring red
and magnified
my shame.

I pined for it so eagerly
that avarice
denied the truth—
so little we covet
means so much
as irretrievable youth!

SHE LOVED NOT ME BUT MY MONEY

She loved not me but my money,
As the keeper not the bee but the honey.
She loved the coins in the well not the wishes,
The pearls in the sea not the fishes.
She loved the song and the dance and the dinner,
But she lied when she called me a winner,
'Cause I'm broke and she's gone and it's funny,
I thought she loved me, not my money.

SHOUT

Voices trapped in silence,
Thoughts taken to the grave,
Feelings locked inside a heart—
The last things you should save.

When you leave they'll wonder
What you might have done,
But their faces will be blank—
For thoughts, you shared not one.

SILVER LINING

Here at the bottom it doesn't get any lower.
The days drag by but can't go any slower.
That's the upside to the downside:
This is as bad as it gets—
The days you remember you tried,
But everyone else forgets.
Rock-bottom is a blessing, not a curse.
Take ease knowing it can't get any worse.

SNOWGLOBE

They keep it so perfect,
the little people living
in the immaculate house,
and I don't know how they do it
or when they find the time,
since I've never actually seen them.

I imagine they peek out through their curtains
and wait for me to turn my back or go to bed
before going outside to replace a light bulb
or repair an upturned shingle,
afraid perhaps that I'll learn their secrets.

How tiny they must be—and smaller yet their tools!
I would love to meet them, but I must admit that
I envy their diligence and dedication to the mundane
whenever I behold my own state of disrepair.

Okay, I'll admit it, I just want to shake them—
turn their whole world upside down
and just shake, shake, shake!

Hmm...maybe they stay inside for other reasons.

SPLIT DECISION

like a boxer
who's taken too many
blows to the head
I sit in my corner
slumped over
punch-drunk and unable
to answer the bell
you loom above me
calling me to the canvas
for one last pummeling
but I can take no more
I can stand no longer
toe-to-toe pretending
it doesn't hurt
there will be
no more bouts
and no more pain
the towel declares you
the winner

STEALING EMILY

At the used-book store,
I hold a copy of *The Complete Poems of*
Emily Dickinson in my hands—
784 pages of economy and eloquence.
But I cannot believe the price,
the ridiculous, laughable price!
One measly dollar—humph!
What a slap in the face—a dollar!
Are you kidding me?
A lifetime of poetic genius for a buck!
I will buy it just to save her the indignation,
even though I already own the book.

But this is not good,
I must have left my wallet at home,
and my pocket change falls well short of fifty cents.
That is why I must steal the copy,
just take it for my own.
Call it professional courtesy—
a risk I am willing to take.
After all, we poets have to stick together.

It's a hefty book—
all those weighty metaphors and deep analogies,
not to mention the sheer volume of the work.
And now I'm not sure how best to conceal its bulk.
So, after much bungling and several glances over my shoulder,
I decide that it's best not to conceal it at all.
I will simply walk out of the store with the confidence of
a man leaving with his own belongings,
a man who has browsed long enough and must be going.

So here we go, the Belle of Amherst and I,
past the poetry and through the maze of fiction,
she becoming acquainted with my sweaty hand,
and I with her squareness and rigid spine.
We meander nonchalantly toward the door,
pausing briefly at its handle, pretending
to take interest in a scandalous headline,
but really just trying to overcome our second thoughts.

But then we have done it,
taken that bold step that moves us into peril,
moves us into that strange but exciting air of the taboo.
And we have gotten away with it, I think,
and I expel a deep and satisfying sigh of relief.
But now the shop owner is pointing at me through the window,
and a young woman is running toward the door.
The blood falls from my face, my heartbeat quickens,
my fight-or-flight reflex tightens to its decision.

I march with hastened steps through the parking lot,
Emily clutched under my arm, close to my chest.
Sir! Sir! Wait! I can hear her shouting.
This is it. I'm caught. I have to stop. I cannot run.
So I turn to face her, my captor, and wait for her reproach.
She is beautiful, smiling and out of breath, young and smooth-
    skinned.
Sir, you dropped your wallet. I dropped my what?
Your wallet. You dropped you wallet. Here.
She hands it to me, and I, looking down at it in disbelief, take it
    from her.

Emily Dickinson. Pardon me? *Emily Dickinson. You like Emily*

Dickinson.
Oh, yes, yes, I do. I stammer. I do like Emily Dickinson.
Me too. She's my favorite. Have a good night.
You too. Thanks for my wallet.
You're welcome. Enjoy Emily.
I will.
I definitely will.

STONE WISDOM

I have concluded—
the stones told me—
that the earth will be here
for a very long time—
long after I am gone,
and histories after you,
whoever you are,
and whatever your agenda.

The vegetation,
however changed,
will as now synthesize the sun,
will reciprocate its lifeblood
to the cumulus and the nimbus,
which in turn will top off the sea
breaking on the shores of Colorado—
and then, a good while later,
on the western shores
of a place once known as New England.

STONES WE'VE THROWN

Because the saint is now a statue
And the martyr now a stone;
Because neither is remembered
Now that centuries have flown;
Because patience is a virtue
That only nature knows;
Because religion is what's popular
And not the work of God;
Because reason is the evolution
Of the executioner's nod.

T.G.I.F.

Fragile is the thread of life,
fleeting is the day,
wasted is the moment spent
wishing time away.

TEATIME DAYDREAM

This is good,
This indefinite adjournment from reality,
This world seen through tracing paper,
These vagaries and figments of clouded vision,
These softened shapes of imperfect focus:
The truth lost and I en route in lengthless pursuit—
Then trumpeted back, startled from a sleepless sleep
To a cold cup of tea.

TEST

There are twenty-two of us in this room.
I'm in the back row and have counted twice.
There are a million other places I'd rather be.

Apart from the drone of the fluorescent lights,
The occasional clearing of a throat, a cough,
Or the scratch of a No. 2 pencil across some paper,

The room is perfectly quiet, perfectly still,
Perfectly detached from the ten-o'clock news,
The history of the world, the poem I wrote last night,
The girl in the coffee shop who flirted with me this morning
Just because I smiled at her...

Section One:

> Q. "If cog A turns clockwise and cog D counterclockwise,
> in which direction does cog C—which is touching cog B,
> which is touching cog A—turn?"

Pistons, viscosity and thermal breakdown,
The wheels grinding to that proverbial halt,
My train of thought derailed in some remote region of the
    Andes—
Are there trains running in the Andes?—
And no one in miles to put me back on track.

At what strange station am I in life?
What if all my cogs fell from their axles,
Clanking their way southward to my medulla oblongata
Where they gathered in a junkyard of forgotten

Three's Company and *Leave it to Beaver* episodes,
Not to mention *M*A*S*H*, *Little House on the Prairie* and
    Laverne and Shirley?
(I wonder if John Boy would have liked Laverne?)

And what if my cogs began to rust because I eat too much salt
And am prone to leaving tools out in the rain?
Surely that wouldn't be good, especially if I found out
Sandblasting wasn't covered under my medical policy.

And what if I jumped up on this table,
Ripped my shirt off and pounded my chest with my fists
In a quick left-right alternating sequence,
Yodeling like Tarzan about to swing off on one of his ever-
    ready vines
To meet Jane or that cute girl in the coffee shop?

That would be good. Yeah, I'd like that.

But someone has squeaked his chair on the floor.
And now the question is rising slowly from the fog of the page,
Its lettered diagram and question gaining clarity in my focusing
    eyes…

    A. Clockwise.

THE ANIMALS SPEAK OF MAN

Why does he torture himself,
Internalizing the inventory of his life,
Obsessed with the credits and debits of his days:
The examination of his conscience:
The scrutiny of his soul?
Isn't it enough for him to be?
Why does he always want more,
Something different?
And why on earth is he afraid to die?
Look out! He's got a gun!

THE AUTHOR'S VISIT

In this dream the author of the book I couldn't finish has come to visit me, come to explain his point of view, and how, if I just give his book another chance, I'll love it—how I'd even recommend it the next time somebody asks me if I've read anything decent lately.

I like his energy, his passion, even as misdirected as it is. I like his hair, too. He looks like a writer, I think. But because he's sitting on my foot, I can't concentrate. I have to keep asking him to repeat himself. He's getting frustrated, and I'm afraid he's going to wake up my wife.

How did he get into the house, I wonder. How did he know which house was mine, or that I bought his book? Why does he care that I couldn't finish it or that I'll probably sell it for ten cents at the garage sale my wife is planning for the first nice Saturday in May?

He asks me if I'm listening, but now my foot is asleep and I'm distracted by my wife's rhythmic snoring. He's not happy and he wants me to go outside with him. When I refuse, he insists, and I'm afraid he's going to get his way. I tell him to relax, that it's just a book, that everything is going to be okay.

Now he's furious, and I don't think he'd get off my foot for anything. So I tell him that I'll give his book a second chance—as soon as I'm done with the others I'm reading. But I'm not convincing enough, and he thinks that I'm lying. And he's right, of course, I'll never finish his book.

He calls me a liar and suddenly grabs me by the collar, rips me from under the covers, drags me downstairs and outside into the street, my bare feet dragging across the lawn, the sidewalk, and then the cold, rough cobblestones. Finally, he drops me and points to my bleeding feet.

See, that's what it's like, he says, when you pour your soul onto a page. It's like a pair of bleeding feet to show the distance you've come. I have no idea what he's talking about, and I tell him that his analogy is lost on me and that he should re-explain himself. But now he's crying and he says that I just don't understand.

He tells me to wait there, in the street, that he'll be right back. I watch him run through the darkness to my neighbor's house. He looks over his left and then his right shoulder, and then climbs through an open window and into the house. A few minutes later, he's returning, dragging my neighbor by his feet.

I must have read further, I think—at least my face is okay. My neighbor is astonished to see me outside this late at night, especially in my pajamas and with bloody feet. I ask him about his face. Just one chapter, he explains. I see, I say, and tell him that I think I read at least four.

And now he's really astonished and wants to know how I did it. I tell him that I'm not sure but ask him if he likes the author's hair. We agree that the style suits him well but that the beard should go. And now the author is exasperated and just shakes his head in disbelief. I remind them about the garage sale and wish them both goodnight.

Back inside I find the author's book and take it upstairs with me. My wife stirs and asks me who I've been talking to. No one, I say, you must have been dreaming. She shivers and tells me that my feet are cold. Turn off the light, honey. You can read your book tomorrow. Okay, I say while yawning, and place the book on the nightstand. You're really going to like it, she says. It's one of the best books I've read.

What did you say? I ask my wife. Umm, she says, nestling into her pillow. I jump out of bed and rush to the window to catch the author, but his back is to me and he's walking away. I slap my palms against the cool glass and call to him. But it's no use. He can't hear me. All I can do is watch as he turns up the collar on his coat, pushes his fists deep into his pockets, and disappears into the thick night fog.

THE BARN

The morning ground-fog, thick and soupy,
Like that spilling over a cauldron's lip,
Swallowed my legs up to my knees
And kept rocks and roots and heaves from view.
Still, I could see the barn off fifty yards or so,
Rising from such deflated clouds as to appear
To be floating in the middle of the sky.

And because I could not rush toward it
For fear of stepping on some pitchfork
Or other tool I should have put away,
I was forced to notice its gray shape,
The handiwork of my father and grandfather:
Its planks evenly planed and spaced
Now warped by sun and rain, thaw and freeze:
Nature's patience twisting out knots and nails alike,
Twisting out a history not even I had seen.

And there, on that cool morning steeped upon me,
The barn, with both of its builders gone,
Stood before me like some revelation:
This is what my father meant when he said—
As his father meant when he said to him—
"Someday, everything you see will be yours."

There, beneath the barn's vanquished pitch,
With its crooked cupola and its tarnished vane
Locked forever north in the wind's usual direction,
I paused, as you do during moments of revelation,
And understood the joy my father must have felt
Knowing that he would live on somehow through me.

And so I stood, like a drop in a spout, trembling there
Until some other force pushed me out of the mystic air.
But the double time of pensive time proved too long:
In the silence I knew the mare had delivered without me.

THE BEAUTIFUL, MERCILESS LADY

Imposter at the end of ale,
In a voice similar to mine:
"What troubles you this eve, dear friend?
From whence grows the vine

"With such a grip about your heart
That tears declare to all your pain?
The night is young and so are you,
And still wholly sane.

"The proffered but rejected heart
Was never remedied by drink;
Nothing but love and passing time
Can ease one from the brink."

I met a lady singular
Of any other I have known,
And she is the Eden-garden
From whence the vine has grown.

To walk within her paradise—
Lush and rife with heavenly fruit,
Teeming with every want of man—
Made all save her seem moot.

I wrote for her true poetry;
She said my pen did grace the page.
She asked for more in confidence;
Would pay me any wage.

A wage? I asked, to pay for what?

She answered only with a sigh.
I would have penned epics for naught,
If given leave to try.

She laughed, and I elated soared;
She wept, and I to see her weep—
A subtle sway within her way
And I did all but sleep.

Until one eve she coaxed my brow
So gently that I slipped to dream
The truth behind the temptress dame
And her deceptive scheme.

Through a mist came scores of poets,
As though arisen from the grave;
They moaned—"The belle has no mercy,
And will make of you a slave!"

Each stood full naked and ashamed;
They had eaten the fruits of hell.
And I awoke to find her gone;
She knew I knew her spell.

And this is my trouble this eve,
Imposter with a voice like mine.
"Come, sit, and I shall pour one more
To drown the evil vine."

THE CARDINAL AND THE WORM

He sang with abandon in his voice,
As he could do only when alone;
And there, unseen, I applauded his choice;
Startled, he turned embarrassed by his tone.

"Please, don't stop because I'm here to hear,
Your song grows sweeter with every note."
But his face grew flushed with a fire to sear
The self-consciousness that clung to his throat.

"Please, sing again, your voice is so sweet,
And I've sore need for a soothing song."
But his eyes stole to something in the street.
I turned to look, turned back, and he was gone.

THE CORD

Now neither spade nor plow will split the ground:
The hog wallow firm and the tire rut stiff;
The pond sealed shut from the tongue of our hound
And the single oar of our fishing skiff.
The ground rejects the seed that spring accepts,
And now as this time every year we praise
The autumn harvest and the faith we kept
When summer drought held the herd from its graze,
For now we reap the rewards of our toil
And the patient fruits of a fallow tract,
Which in a season replenished its soil
With strength to grow if not power to act.
    All this I think, my palms pressed to the glow
    Of pine split and corded one year ago.

THE DIMINISHED PUPIL

He chalks his problems on the board
Until he blinds himself with white;
Then night erases yesterday
And sleep makes things all right.

But day renews so he again
Searches for answers to his whys
In a scribbled web of questions
He lets ensnare his eyes.

And so it goes for the scholar
In a circle of night and day,
Until better sense comes to him
When thought is put away.

THE GAMBLER'S LAMENT

ROULETTE
Bet all of your money on red.
Bet all of your money on black.
Bet all of your money that you will lose
And you might make your money back.

BLACKJACK
Split your aces and your eights.
Count your bullets as eleven or one.
But if your cards read twenty or less
You still lose to twenty-one.

SLOTS
Nickels, quarters, dollars—
The one-armed bandits love them all.
Those reels will keep on spinning
Until you haven't a dime for a call.

THE GRASS UPON THE BATTLEFIELD

Before these towers stood to fall,
Before these plumes of grief and pall
'Wakened a land detached from fact
To the same sun shone upon all,

The grass grew green upon this tract,
The sea broke on a shore yet sacked
By men and gods and difference:
A land still green to what it lacked.

But soon they came to build their fence—
As empires with the same pretense—
To guard their ways from those afield
With views their own on providence.

It matters not what might men wield,
Before which gods they may have kneeled,
We see what all the ages yield:
Grass green upon the battlefield.

THE INCOMPLETE WORKS, PLEASE

Will someone get rich from my works when I'm dead,
publishing a book with the words *The Complete Works*
in the title? After all, I'm a poet, and it seems the most
successful poets are those decomposing composers
who had fair success while alive but fame after passing.
Why is it this way? I think that perhaps it's because
poets speculate about the afterlife, enter it, and thereby
attract the morbid fascination of those less articulate
thinkers now wondering if the poets had it right.
So to all would-be buyers of a someday-dead poet's poems,
do me a favor and buy my books now, while I'm alive,
because I could really use the money. Besides, trust me,
there isn't a poet dead or alive with any more of an idea
about what happens when we die than you or I.

THE MAGIC WORD

"Get me some chips, mama"
comes the directive from our three-year-old.
"Excuse me? What's the magic word?"
asks my wife with her routine reminder for politeness.
 "Abracadabra," comes the response,
followed by the laughter of two very proud parents.

THE ONLY WAY I'LL GET TO HEAVEN

Yes, I said of the light beaming from my eyes,
it is from the swallowed halo.
I must admit too that the feathers on my tongue
are from the angel's wings.
You have to come with us, They said,
and They led me away in golden shackles.

THE PUBLISHER WANTS

to tap into my mind,
like a screw through a cork,
each turn twisting deeper,
closer to the blood
that sustains the buzz
of the fly, he seems to me,
an avid pest of little worth,
whose advance deserves a swat,
a good smack across the face,
or at least a good talking-to.

THE PARADOX OF SOCKS

Seam-side-in or seam-side-out,
Which way to wear your socks?
Is fashion king and comfort out,
The question a paradox?

THE QUIET MUSIC OF MADNESS

They arrested him in the park,
where the western edge bends to meet the river
under the stand of hundred-year-old maples.
His bare feet wet with morning dew,
he was not about to run away.

They approached him from behind,
their fingers far from their guns,
and asked him, with grins on their faces,
to stop playing his violin so that
they could ask him some questions.
"Sir, where are your clothes?"
"Sir? Sir, please put the violin down."

Later, in the back of the cruiser,
his violin in the trunk,
he sat draped in a blue blanket,
oblivious to the onlookers
and the audience of two in the front seat:
Eyes closed,
ear bent to shoulder,
fingers pressing invisible strings,
the unseen bow dragging out
the quiet music of madness.

THE RIGHT WAY TO HOLD A FORK

An infraction of the highest kind,
to hold your fork incorrectly.
The etiquette police take notice with their disbelieving eyes,
but they have no powers of arrest,
they have only the power to criticize,
only the power to squirm in the seats of their scrutiny,
uncomfortable in the presence of such rudeness,
such ill-mannered behavior.
Oh how I enjoy the discomfort of the pretentious!
And up next, a bowlful of soup without a spoon.
Here, allow me to show you where to stick that fork!

THE SIX RESTRAINTS

I

Pride, you pebble in my shoe,
I could run with anyone
If I'd but stop to clear you.

II

Guilt, you hiccup in my heart,
I could shame the weight of blame
If I'd but admit my part.

III

Greed, you serpent in my gut,
I could quell the debts of hell
If I'd but give up my glut.

IV

Lust, you prize for which I pine,
I could win what fortunes spin
If I'd but value what's mine.

V

Fear, you blind over my eyes,
I could brave even my grave
If I'd but remove your guise.

VI

Hate, you head upon my shelf,
I could spurn what epochs learn
If I'd but think for myself.

THE THIRD CANDIDATE

Buckets filled with dampened sand—
Patted, smoothed, flipped, tapped.
A castle begins to take shape.
The laborers and foremen, six and seven,
Brothers working in rare cooperation
Under a mid-August sun on a cloudless day,
Dig a moat with their earnest hands—
And the castle is complete.
But who will be king of this New World?
Who is best suited to lead and to rule?
The argument begins; the wrestling match ensues,
Each declaring he is king.
But while they fight they are blind to see
A Third Candidate rising up from the sea
With ideas His own on sovereignty.
With a single autocratic blow,
The Third Candidate assumes undisputed rule.
The boys, startled and slack-jawed on the sand,
Watch helplessly while their empire melts in His hands.

THE TIGHTROPE OF REGRET

You have done this before. We all have. You know you are about to do something you will regret, but you do it anyway—in spite of your father's voice in the back of your head reminding you that you always learn things the hard way, just like he did, just like we all do.

You say *I do*, *I will*, *I hate you*, *I love you*. You buy it, sell it, eat it or drink it. You say *yes* or you say *no*. Then you hate yourself, cannot believe how stupid you are for doing what you knew you should not have done. But, like the tightrope walker who has had too much coffee, you have to give the crowd what it wants.

THE TRUTH ABOUT THE PAST

The camera winks its cycloptic eye at me
As if to say, "We're all set here, buddy.
Got just the right amount of light to capture the moment.
You can go on with your life now."

But I feel cheated somehow,
As if a piece of my life has been stolen,
Albeit just a shot, just a frame in time.

I know it's behind me,
But no matter which way I turn I can't see it;
I can't recapture the pose or the contrived smile.

I clutch at the air to pull the irretrievable into the present.
But the moment has been swallowed,
And I can't gag the past with my finger down its throat
To force its ever-expanding stomach to loose
And spill its guts at my feet
So that I can stir elbow-deep in a pool of time,
Fishing in a million moments for the one that got away,
The one I want again.

It's useless,
So I turn my attention to the camera,
Rip the roll of memory from its body,
Hold it to the light, search for the frame,
And in turn expose the truth about the past:
You can never get it back.

THE VERY END

The last bubble warbles to the surface,
pops in the crisp air of oblivion,
ripples to a shrinking edge, and is gone.

The last wind struggles up a crumbling mountain,
succumbs to the last ounce of gravity,
and tumbles like a weary climber to its death.

The last flame sputters in the last whit of wax,
crackles, spits, hisses and dies.
The smoke dissipates into nothing.

The last cloud sinks into the sea.
The earth soaks up the sea.
The universe swallows the earth.

And in the end, the very end,
a hand reaches around a corner, gropes along a wall,
finds the switch, and turns out the light.

THIS IS LIKE TALKING TO MY WIFE

I like this stanza already
Because I know where it's going—
Although I haven't told you yet.

Since I didn't get to the point
In the opening stanza,
Allow me to try here in the second...

Sorry about that.
I should have chosen longer stanzas
Because this is already the end of the third

And I haven't even come close to making my point.
But here in the fourth
I think I know how I can do it in the fifth.

At last, here we are in the fifth and final stanza
And now I can finally get to my point:
Now you understand the title.

TO NEW ENGLAND FROM ENGLAND

To New England from England we came reluctantly,
my two sisters and I, pieces of our mother's baggage.
For me it was simple: I would wait for the sea to freeze
before I set out without fear of sharks back to England—
I wasn't foolish, I knew the distance was too far to swim.
That winter I waited by the shore in irredeemable cold
for the Atlantic tide to slow and eventually stop.
But it never did, and later I learned that it never had
and never would.

TOO MUCH SAKI

as green as the grass
on the moon at noon
it's sunday
in tokyo
there's no fishin' here
the sign's quite clear
it's cold as hell
and the heat doth swell
when you drive your car
to earth's first star
for a cold lemonade
in the hot-damn shade
of tokyo, yes, tokyo
there's a zero near
you hear in your ear
with a swat at a gnat
with your new straw hat
from tokyo, yes, tokyo

TWENTY-FIRST-CENTURY ANTS

The ants have found a curious sand from which to build their tunneled homes—whole piles of it—light and white and sweet, their answer to the honeycomb. But production isn't going well, it seems they're feasting as they go, and in the orgy of their senses have turned happy, fat, and slow. And overhead a cloud lets loose the deluge of its fill, and the curious sand melts in their hands and washes away with their will.

UPON RETURNING

Upon returning to elementary school
Thirty years after I left it behind for junior high,
I could not believe how they had done it:
How they had miniaturized everything,
Shrunken the desks and the chairs down
To play things, to models of the real thing;
How they had scaled back the hallways,
Narrowed the once vast canyons in which,
As a boy, I grew restless waiting for my echo
To return the *hello* I offered to one end;
How I could now extend my arms and touch
At once both sides with my fingertips.
How I stood there marveling my bigness,
The enormity of my existence,
The incredible distance I had come,
And the unknown distance yet to go.

USED GOODS

I sold the world
but it wasn't mine to sell
oh well
there's a sucker at every turn
who wants it easy
who wants it cheap
who wants what he can't have
but I am there to sell it to him
anyway
secondhand

VENI, VIDI, VEGGIE
(I came, I saw, I had salad)

Valet parking, tie required—
Damn! My credit card expired!

VERSE SCIOLTI DA RIMA

Really now, what is a cemetery
but little more than a human junkyard,
a depot for departed humankind,
a collection of decomposing parts
cataloged and noted on marble cards
for every visitor whose parts still work.
Or perhaps a cemetery is more
a department store for window shoppers
whose sole intention is to imagine
having the goods the marble cards describe.
Or maybe a cemetery is less
a department store and more a warehouse,
a storage facility for excess
merchandise for which there is no shelf space.
Or yet still perhaps a cemetery
is nothing more than a history book
written on grass pages and stone covers,
a preservation of past lives, past times.
Or maybe a cemetery is more
a bank that only allows deposits—
no withdrawals, no loans, no interest.
Or perhaps a cemetery is more
a museum with descriptive placards
for exhibits no longer on display.
Or maybe it is a convention hall
to which everybody is invited
but nobody knows when or where or how.
Perhaps it is all this and much, much more.
Perhaps it is none of this, none of this at all.

VITA BREVIS

Today's already yesterday,
and tomorrow's already come,
so I just pray and make my way
with my back turned toward the sun.

I know the place all runners come;
it's not to any far away.
But there's a distance none can run:
nothing's as far as yesterday.

W.B.

My foe outstretched beneath the tree,
Piping songs of pleasant glee,
Warbled out these metres meet...
And when thy heart began to beat
They clothed me in the clothes of death:
He had forgiven my final breath.

WAITING

It is a peculiarity of man that he can only live by looking to the future—sub specie aeternitatis.
                              —Victor Frankl

Indeed, Mr. Yeats, man has created death.
He too has created all the measurements of life,
against which he holds himself accountable,
considers himself a success or a failure,
considers where he is and where he wants to be.
And when he prays he prays to himself,
he prays for the appeasement of his conscience.
His pride is his invention; his ego his bane.
Greed, jealousy and selfishness are all his own.
No other animal knows such contrivances:
No other animal waits for death.

WALKING THE DOG

my dog wants to walk
but I've been so bad in my life
I've hurt
promised
lied
stolen
cheated
denied
my dog wants to walk
but I've been so bad in my life

WAR'S OTTAVA RIMA

Only the dead have seen the end of war.
—Plato

Above, below, the ages go,
For neither good nor evil stays:
The leaf above the root below
Gives umbrage from the eye of days
But cannot stop a season's snow
From falling down in frozen glaze
Upon the cross joined to the row
Of fallen men in early graves.
    Above, below, the ages bide—
    Yet still we kill like none has died.

WE TWO LONELY FOOLS

Eheu fugaces labuntur anni. — Alas! The fleeting years glide on.

I avert my eyes and purposely deprive my senses out of fear that what I see here will awaken in me something that we shared long ago, for we both know that urgent longing unclaimed but belonging to two fools too daft to sail the craft was more than a feeling of our senses reeling and rather a chance for two fools to dance. But in spite that it's short we've made life a sport and ignored the rift ever growing between doing and knowing. So again it's good-bye, though neither knows why, but these are the rules of we two lonely fools.

WEEP FOR ME NO MORE

Weep for me no more, though sorrow's so dear
A friend as one awakened at midnight
To ease your troubles with a softened ear:
Grief that lingers long consumes you outright.
Lips kissed yours 'fore mine touched even your cheek;
Should they be the last to hold your sweet kiss,
Then robbed be all men of the love they seek,
And you with but memories of such bliss.
'Tis true to the wind my flame lost the fight—
Aye, 'tis true that every flame will succumb—
But you, though there be wick enough to light,
Cut short your days before they should be done:
   If for your life such darkness will suffice,
      Then know, dear, that I died not once but twice.

WHAT DOES HUMAN SAY?

        chirp
        oink
        roar
        bleat
        how
        does
        human
        speak?
        hiss
        howl
        moo
        bray
        what
        does
        human
        say?
        meow
        caw
        quack
        tweet
        how
        does
        human
        speak?
        croak
        woof
        yip
        neigh
        what
        does
        human
        say?

WHAT THE EARTH IS WORTH

Though trees be mighty, tall, and strong;
Though the years be many, and long,
It is Mother Earth and her soil
That give birth to the bluebird's song.

To the trees the Earth stays loyal—
Though wind and rain do often toil
And try to down the mighty trees
That give shade when the sun does boil.

And She holds true through melt and freeze
To what roots alone could not breathe
Or give birth to a mighty girth
Made for swinging a lofty breeze.

Who can say what the Earth is worth—
A thousand times a human mirth?
Or be a million times a dearth
Compared to what the Earth is worth?

WHEN I AM DEAD
(a parody of Christina Rossetti's *When I Am Dead*)

When I am dead, my sweetheart,
    Throw a party for me—
Well, not really for me, my love,
    But in my memory.
Invite my drunken friends, dear,
    And pour for each an ale,
And keep their glasses full, dear,
    Until their legs all fail.

I shall not mind the mess, love,
    I shall not fear the strain
From rooms of pie-eyed friends, dear,
    Singing as if in pain.
Take their keys and if you please
    Give aspirin for each head—
But tell them to live now, dear,
    For soon they too are dead.

WHEN SHE'S ONLY BEAUTIFUL

Remember that the most beautiful things in the world are the most useless; peacocks and lilies, for example.
— John Ruskin

Skin-deep,
That's what they say about beauty,
That superficial magnet to which one is drawn—
Pulled, in fact, involuntarily by that which in us is animal:
The unalterable and undeniable instinct of attraction.

The truth, though, is that the visceral rarely lasts;
It hardly ever sustains us long enough to matter.
And that is the dilemma of man's duality:
To be at once animal and unanimal,
Civilized and uncivilized.

I could say that beauty fades and that love lasts,
Or that fancy is fleeting and that love endures,
But we've heard all of that before.
We know the difference between the ideal and the real,
And still we can't deny what's elemental in us all.

I'll say instead, then, that life, to me, is about the pursuit of
    moments;
That the years teach much which the days never know.
And while each of us teeters on the tightrope of our nature,
Struggling with our contrivance and our self-imposed,
Remember that real beauty cannot be touched, it can only be
    felt.

WHEN TO REST WE LAY THE WORLD'S SWAY

When to rest we lay the world's sway,
One never knows what dreams may come
In the slumber of parting day.

Sleep unsheathes us as blocks of clay
And wheels in turn our conscience numb,
When to rest we lay the world's sway.

With inhibitions put away,
We fall as in an ether numb
In the slumber of parting day.

Shaped and fired in a dream we slay
That to which by day we succumb,
When to rest we lay the world's sway.

Sleep takes us where we'd never stray—
Aware and under our own thumb—
In the slumber of parting day.

If as in dreams awake we'd stay!
We'd needn't dream to mask the glum
When to rest we lay the world's sway
In the slumber of parting day.

DEATH ON PARSON'S POND

The angles of the winter sun,
Low and sharp and bright,
Have the power of a midyear's torch for giving light.
Yet at the close of year and with the new of next,
It is as if they are by some veil vexed,
For their rays arrive but too their frost,
And while light remains its warmth is lost:
The leaves succumb, the blades turn brown,
The water wears its frozen crown,
And winter creeps into our little town.

On etching blades the townies score
Their hour into the icy floor of Parson's Pond,
Where the glass stretches to the banks and beyond.
Among them lovers new and old,
My untouched tea gone cold,
I dream of when we would glide upon that body's broken tide,
When you were young and so was I,
Before your wings were given to fly;
Before I knew this unshakeable chill
For what is lost but wanted still.

A crime to which no townsman confessed,
They found you ravaged and barely dressed
In Parson's Pond, the tender reeds among,
Your hair still turned in golden tress.
And on that eve the year's first frost
Besieged my heart with untold cost:
The just burden of the unjustly jailed,
So be your safety the job I failed.
And failed, too, this wintry light
At warming your lover's eternal night.

WORDS OF INSPIRATION FROM A SAOP OPERA STAR

Listen, all my children, these are the days of our lives, and we have but one life to live as the world turns. Although you are the young and the restless, you too are the bold and the beautiful. Let your passions be your guiding light and they will lead you to another world!

X SPEAKS

The Boomers' babies paid for tomorrow's hit parade,
Unwittingly securing their parents' social status—
But the milk ran dry and the honey went by—
Devoured by the hunger of those who begat us.

CONSCIENCE

If I travel on the wings of the morning,
If I hide in the darkness of night,
I cannot escape my conscience—
Everything is exposed,
Every work brought into judgment,
Every action manifest again.
I cannot outrun my shadow.
I cannot hide from myself.

TRUST

How is a building built, son?
Brick upon brick.
And how is it destroyed, son?
One quake will do the trick.
And what about trust, son?
Ah! Papa, the very same way.

THE LAZARUS EFFECT

Lacking genuine virtue, the unthinking man
Mired in the subservience of his religion,
Compulsory and concoctive as it is,
Is contented in self-wrought unawareness
By the swapping of deliberate action
For the ceremonial and deferential.

How can he, unworthy and born into sin,
Bound to law yet fettered to doctrine,
Fawning over a hateful god invented
To assuage his sense of mortality,
Give credence to an idol utter?

Absolved through tithe and ritual
By a god not held to mutual scrutiny,
To himself made unaccountable through rite,
The man propped up by the crux of his religion—
His promise of everlasting life—
Has betrayed his humanness to become a puppet
Upon strings controlled by the equally deceived—
The equally damned.

He is led himself astray by historical self-deception
Into that grotto of startling revelation—
That he, after all the hollow promises,
Is accorded the same death as the pismire
Or the sacrificial lamb slaughtered upon the altar floor
As a gift for his death-loving god.

Oh, poor children, whose ears let in the ruse
Whispered at such a corruptible age;

Whose natural reverence and awe of life
Is diminished if not destroyed by the ideals
Of those who have forgotten innocence;
Of those who have entrusted their fate
To the contrivance of religious ideology:
You have become both the duped and the dupers.

Posit as you may the virgin doxy
In the ineffable name of Jehovah!
You are Judas, Judas left holding the bag of betrayal.
You are Lazarus, Lazarus who died anyway.

A POEM WRITTEN IN THREE-LETTER WORDS BEGINNING WITH O

Off one odd oak oar,
Our own oat ort out,
Old owl oft oe'r—ooh!

YOU, ROBERT FROST

Bob, can I get a hand here, please?
This wall is as much yours as it is mine, you know.
And what makes a good neighbor is not a wall but a hand,
And I'd like to keep *my* promises, too.

Here's a directive for you:
Come down from that poor birch tree—
You look like an absolute idiot swinging around up there,
And help me mend this stupid wall.
That would make all the difference to *me*.

Come on, Robert—out! out!
You're really starting to piss me off!
Put your silly poetry away
Before we're *both* acquainted with the night,
And help me mend this goddamned wall!

CLOSING ILLNESS

I've listened to a rusted hinge
Moan out its lament,
And thankful that the door it swings
Is so seldom bent.

I know what lies beyond that door.
Yes, I know the pain—
That door has opened twice before,
And closed twice the same.

And now before it rests a third
Hand upon its latch,
Stricken with that closing illness
All the living catch.

A BEGINNER'S GUIDE TO CREATING A RELIGION

1. Create a god.
2. Convince yourself that your god is real.
3. Bow down to your god and fear its power.
4. Learn to hate and even kill those who do not believe in your god.

(Note: If you have trouble with steps three and four, go back to step two.)

I LIKE SHORT POEMS BEST

I like short poems best,
The ones that in their brevity
Still impart that contemplative *hmmm*,
Those poems proportionate to
The span of my attention;
My disposition's deficit.

IF I LIVE TO SEE TOMORROW

If I live to see tomorrow
I'll do what I should've done today,
But I know that tomorrow
Again you'll hear me say:
If I live to see tomorrow
I'll do what I should've done today,
But I know that tomorrow
Again you'll hear me say...

EVOLUTIUON, BABY!

Vertigo from the ladder's top rung,
I wait for the wood to rot—
I wait for evolution to eat me!

AFTER PANGAEA

Everything was one once.
The mountains didn't need a name,
They were just the mountains.
There were no continents, no countries,
No territories, no provinces, no states.
But that was long ago, long before division,
Long before difference and distinction,
Long ago but just before we arrived.
Now there is no Pangaea;
Now the lands are many;
Now the people are persons.

PACKING THE POETS

Milton doesn't mind the darkness at the bottom of the box; not surprising, considering how half his light was spent. Shakespeare, however, squirms between the selfsame darkness of the book-covers, but doesn't speak, silently admitting resistance is folly. Next is Shelley, also a squirmer. He, like Prometheus, would like to be unbound but is relegated instead to the mere memory of a West Wind that will never drive apart his bindings. Keats and Byron complete the triangle. The three of them musing over their halfhearted embrace of Negative Capability, *perhaps this too will be a pleasure to look back on one day—forsan et haec olim meminisse juvabit.* Bukowski tells the three of them to shut the fuck up and deal with it; tells Shelley that he's a pussy and that his wife had bigger balls than he did. *Fucking Romantics! Speak English!* Dickinson is mortified and pretends to count bees that aren't really there. Frost reminds them all that he has promises to keep and miles to go before he sleeps, which reminds Whitman that he made A Promise to California. Chaucer is confused and wants to ask Bukowski what *fuck* means and why he referred to Shelley as a cat, but he's blocked by Pound's Cantos and Eliot's Waste Land. Then comes Tennyson, who mumbles shyly to Byron that he's not the only Lord in the box. Next is Blake, unafraid of the darkness with his Tyger burning bright, followed by Rossetti—the sister—Marvell, Pope, and then Arnold. Now, with room for just one more poet, the venerable Yeats rounds out the pack, nudges Eliot as if to remind him with no insidious intent that he's not the only Nobel winner in the bunch. Rossetti calls for her brother, but he's already in another box, rubbing elbows with the likes of Wordsworth, Browning, Plath, Jonson and Hunt, all of whom, as I, admire Bryant's Thanatopsis and wish they had written such a masterpiece at just seventeen. Divorcing my wife of seven years, I prepare to leave the narrow house and take the poets with me.

BROKEN GLASS

The audacity of the petulant
bitch called my mother!
Now with a dowager's hump
and a bronchial hack,
The gifts of her insidious disease—
her regimen of
Wild Turkey and Marlboro Lights—
she preaches to me
the morals she never had.
(How dare you evangelize
the mutterings of family,
O Great Abandoner,
woman I love,
after all.)

Still, in spite of her
misdirected misery turned inside
out, like a coat with some incriminating
letter she wishes to hide,
I imagine her as a little girl
running through a field of gold
with a pailful of possibilities,
oblivious to the tiny hole
through which her future
seeps until the hole is stopped
up with the aging sludge
of pessimism, indifference,
and incurable self-pity.
The pile of stones and the glass
walls are far too enticing.

TODAY'S POETRY

It's all about the line-
breaks. The double entendre
enjambment hell-bent on saying
more than it can or should. You
read only to reread, to
try to understand what goes
with what. The poem is
trying to speak, I know it!

ALMOST

To come close, to be right there, with the end in sight...
The oasis never reached but the mirage still glimmering,
Still shimmering in the unattainable distance,
Like the pot of gold at the *other* end of the fading rainbow.
Some things sought are not worth seeking.

ONANISTIC INTERLUDE
(a play with one part)

tangerine
juice on a tongue—
shining star
rays flung
on a boy
who dreams of someone—

moisture forms
on parts he knows well—
keep it up—
you know he'll never tell
anyone
of this welcome spell

nectar flows
to be swallowed down—
ruby lips
on a purple crown—
the erect king
of his own little town

job in hand—
clenched in a fist—
squeezing out
a reality missed—
a fantasy spun
with a cockeyed wrist

time has come
to hold back a scream—

ride the waves
of a pearl-white stream—
swimming again
in a tangerine dream

ZERO TO YOU IN TEN SECONDS

Zero in on the one and only who makes two company and three a crowd—unless you're a musketeer, in which case you'll have to travel to the four corners of the world to take five before you're at sixes and sevens and really behind the eight ball deciding if cloud nine is a perfect ten!

ARMS AND LEGS

There are many kinds of arms and legs,
not just those familiar appendages
with which we walk or wield a watch.
There's no need to go out on a limb.
Arms are in fact quite far-reaching,
and legs step well beyond the bound
of a limited stride that needs repeating
to reach a distance worth a measure.
Consider the endurance of table legs,
for example. They never need to rest.
The arms of a chair are never flexed,
yet theirs is a muscle stronger than flesh.
They have an anatomy with real strength.
Take a coat of arms and contemplate
its symbolism and silent history.
There's a story there—possibly an epic.
The proliferation of small arms is big, too,
but fortunately there's the long arm of the law.
Not too many things reach farther.
And there's the last leg of a race
and the final leg of a journey,
and you may think you have a leg up
on the competition, but when it comes
to arms and legs of a different kind,
believe me, you don't have a leg to stand on.

SPACE

Space is quite perplexing.
Forget outer space,
I'm talking about earthly space.
Where does it go when my body fills it?
Is it like the mathematical zero,
Nothing more than a placeholder?
Am I simply filling it or have I displaced it,
Like the water in my bath when I bathe?
Has earth's atmosphere popped out somewhere
In the exact proportion of my being
To accommodate the space I've taken up,
Sidling along the celestial body with every step I take?
Maybe space is as vacuous as this contemplation?
Perhaps its only dimension is the one
Proportionate to the size of the headache
I get when asking such stupendously stupid questions.
Space, after all, is only what's there when I'm not.

BOUYS

While the party danced on without me,
I strode out into the cool evening air
Under a Milky Way blanket shimmering
On the cold black Atlantic coast of Maine,
A slow throbbing of buoy bells
Lamenting in the distance.
No one had noticed, I thought,
Until a tender and familiar hand
Wove its silken fingers into mine.
My little girl, a radiant young woman,
Standing there in her wedding dress,
Wiped away the tear I was trying to hide:
"I love you, daddy. Please come back inside."

THE LAST LAUGH

Time is constant.
It laughs at me
When I think I'll live forever.
But I write
And I write
And I just might
Have the last laugh.

Index of titles and first lines...
(First lines appear in italics)

1. CREATE A GOD.	569
A BARREL, A BUSHEL	*132*
A BEGINNER'S GUIDE TO CREATING A RELIGION	569
A BETTER NEIGHBOR	154
A CAROUSEL OF DAYS	362
A CASE FOR WILLN'T	363
A CHILD ISN'T BORN AFRAID OF THE DARK.	*415*
A CLAMMY HANDSHAKE	*335*
A CONVERSATION WITH MY FATHER	114
A DAY'S WORTH OF SNIPPETS	50
A DEAD SOLDIER SPEAKS	364
A DECORATED SOLDIER	223
A FARMER SURVIVED	96
A FATHER IS TOLD THAT HIS SON IS DEAD, AND THEN TOLD HE	4
A FISTFUL	*281*
A FLICKER SCATTERS A MIST.	*406*
A FLY FORETELLS OF WINTER	365
A FRIEND'S ATTENTION	366
A GUN DOES NOT A KILLER MAKE	*160*
A GUY SAYS TO ME	5
A HISS, A DRIP, A DROP	*158*
A HITHERTO UNKNOWN CHILD	*79*
A JUMP FROM REASON	256
A LITTLE MADNESS	367
A LONG WAY TO THE MOON ON A FERRY	*355*
A MAN SWALLOWS HARD.	*324*
A MEAGER SEED	274
A METICULOUS MAN WAS HE	*2*
A MURDER OF CROWS	*359*
A NEW WEIGHT-LOSS PROGRAM	368

A PARENT'S PRAYER FOR A CHILD SOLDIER	310
A PINION IN THE SUN	*401*
A PLUMMETING MAN	*146*
A POCKED ELLIPSE	302
A POEM WRITTEN IN THREE-LETTER WORDS BEGINNING	566
A RECIPE FOR RESTAURANTS	132
A RENTAL TRUCK FILLED WITH FERTILIZER	6
A SEASIDE GIFT	369
A SELFISH MOTHER	247
A SLIVER OF A BOY	*142*
A SUN UNTO ITSELF	*32*
A TALE TWICE TOLD	238
A TEASE	141
A TETHERED EMBRYO	*372*
A THIRD PARTY	370
A THREE-LEGGED DOG NAMED HOOVER	7
A UNIQUE FLOWER	309
A VOICE FOR CHANGE	318
A WILD DOG—ANY ONE—LICKS ITS WOUNDS	*479*
A WOMAN'S WORK	236
A WOMAN'S CHOICE	372
A WORD WITHHELD WORKS A WONDER	*3*
A WORD WITHHELD	3
A YOUNG PRESIDENT	8
ABOVE, BELOW, THE AGES GO	*551*
ACCOUNTABLE	304
AFLUTTER IS THE RAINBOW	*393*
AFTER A HOUSE OF CARDS	294
AFTER BROTHER CALLED	*303*
AFTER PANGAEA	573
AH! TO POSTULATE	*181*
ALL I AM IS ALL I KNOW	173
ALMOST	577

ALONG A STONY SEASIDE PATH	*369*
AM I SO BANISHED FROM THESE DARK WALLS	*285*
AM I TIME'S MASTER OR IT MINE?	*197*
AMADEUS	*264*
AMERICA, AMERICA	*300*
AN ENEMY OUTRIGHT	*374*
AN EPIC IN A SENTENCE	*194*
AN EXAMPLE OF INARGUABLE LOGIC	*375*
AN INFRACTION OF THE HIGHEST KIND	*532*
AND TALK ABOUT THE WEATHER	*88*
AND THE PEOPLE	*376*
AND YOU THOUGHT TRIGONOMETRY WAS HARD	*237*
ANTICONFESSIONAL	*377*
APOCALYPTIC REVERSAL	*305*
ARGUMENT	*378*
ARMS AND LEGS	*581*
ARTHUR, MY FIFTY-TWO-POUND BEAGLE	*13*
AS A CHILD I WONDERED	*121*
AS A CHILD, FOOTLOOSE AND FANCY-FREE	*200*
AS A MAN SO LEAVES HIS YOUTH	*379*
AS A, LIKE A, AS A, LIKE A	*71*
AS FADED AS A WINTER ROSE	*471*
AS GREEN AS THE GRASS	*541*
AS I WAS YOUNG AND FATHERLESS	*381*
AS I WAS YOUNG	*381*
AS RESTLESS AS A CHIHUAHUA ON SPEED	*198*
ASHES TO ASHES, DIAPERS TO DIAPERS	*383*
ASKED TO WRITE A POEM FOR FRIENDS	*481*
AT HER OWN HAND	*384*
AT LAST MY FATHER IS WISE	*168*
AT THE CONVENTION OF PAST TYRANTS AND GENERALS	*327*
AT THE EDGE OF INNOCENCE	*251*
AT THE SAME TIME I WAS LEARNING HOW TO RIDE A BIKE	*465*

AT THE USED-BOOK STORE	504
ATTITUDE PLATITUDE	385
AUTUMNAL REVELATION	386
BANISHED	285
BE AN ENEMY OUTRIGHT	374
BE MY SUMMERS BEREFT	229
BE STILL, LILY	286
BE THE AUTHOR OF YOUR LIFE	226
BECAUSE I AROSE BEFORE YOU	387
BECAUSE I LIVED	174
BECAUSE LOVE IS ROUND	213
BECAUSE THE SAINT IS NOW A STATUE	508
BECAUSE	387
BEFORE IT'S TOO LATE	263
BEFORE THESE TOWERS STOOD TO FALL	525
BET ALL OF YOUR MONEY ON RED	524
BETWEEN THE LINES	388
BEWILDERED, AS A MAN CAN BE	212
BEYOND ICE	389
BIBLE AND BIG BANG	192
BIBLE SALES	390
BIRD FLU	391
BLACK, STRETCH WITH THE SUN	320
BLESS THE MONK WHO WAKES WITH AN ERECTION.	237
BLISS?	184
BOB, CAN I GET A HAND HERE, PLEASE?	567
BODY LANGUAGE	392
BONE UPON BONE	12
BOUYS	583
BRAINKEEPING	177
BREATHLESS IN MAINE	94
BROKEN GLASS	575
BRUSH STROKES	126

BUCKETS FILLED WITH DAMPENED SAND.. *535*
BURN VICTIM 313
BUTTERFLY 393
BY SIGHT BUT NOT SOUND 394
CAFFEINE AND CONSCIENCE 219
CALLING TO ARTHUR 13
CAN WE NOT GET TO THE HEART OF THE MATTER?.................................. 75
CAN'T SEE THE BOTTOM. *354*
CANDLE'S CLIME 163
CARNIVAL SEVENTEEN 14
CARPE DIEM 15
CASTAWAYS.. 395
CHIRP... *554*
CLIMBING WITH NO FOOTHOLD.. *185*
CLOSING ILLNESS 568
CLOSING VOYAGE 228
CLOUDS HAVE BECOME CLOUDS.. *47*
COFFEE SHOP CADENCE 158
COLLATERAL DAMAGE 396
COLLISION 397
COMET 234
COMET, WITH YOUR TAIL STREAMING *234*
COMING BACK AS A BUG 398
CONSCIENCE 562
CONSECRATED CHURCH OF YORE *323*
CONSIDERING HE WAS SUPPOSED TO BE IN PRISON 22
CONVERSATION CLOSED 233
COOL IN MY GARDEN'S *186*
CORN 16
CORPUS CALLOSUM 399
CRACKED... *307*
CURRENT EVENTS ARE HIGHLY OVERRATED. *452*
CUT UP EVERY BATTLESHIP.. *69*

DAMN THIS SNOW!	271
DAWN BY THE RIVER.	*31*
DEATH AT SEA	400
DEATH BY A THOUSAND CUTS	18
DEATH IN THE DESERT	401
DEATH ON PARSON'S POND	559
DEATH	359
DEATHLESS LOVE	259
DEEP IN THE FOG	*116*
DÉJÀ VU TWO	402
DÉJÀ VU	170
DEPARTED FLOWER	282
DERAILED TRAIN OF THOUGHT	317
DESCRIBING A RAINBOW TO A BLIND MAN	19
DIFFERENCE QUANTIFIED	20
DIGITAL MAN	242
DISGUSTED	334
DISSOLVE	167
DISTRACTED BY A PRETTY WAITRESS	403
DIVINITY	21
DIVORCE COURT	353
DO YOU KNOW WHY WE TELL YOU TO TURN	*70*
DOES IT MATTER WHAT TODAY IS LIKE	*88*
DONE	404
DRAW THOSE CURTAINS AND CLOSE THAT DOOR	*118*
DREADED WASH DAY	*112*
DRINKING FROM A CHAMBER POT.	*433*
DRIVING WITH THE MAGIC MAN	*405*
DULL THE MIND AND THICK.	*230*
DURING THE PROUDEST MOMENTS OF MY LIFE.	*78*
DUTY	406
EACH DAY THE WORLD GETS SMALLER	*171*
EACH IS ENDOWED A CANVAS CLEAN.	*126*

ECHOES OF EMILY	23
ECONOMICS 101: THE NEED TO EAT, AKA THE REASON	407
EGOISTS	408
EMILY'S IN THE ATTIC	272
EMPTY HEARTS CANNOT REFRAIN	*169*
ENAMORED IS THE MAN	*151*
ESPECIALLY BOURBON	99
ET TU	409
EVER FEEL LIKE IT'S ALL ABOUT YOU	*61*
EVERY DAY A BLACKENED SOUL	*331*
EVERY DAY AT FIVE	189
EVERY MAN HAS A SHARE	*182*
EVERY MAN SHOULD KNOW HUNGER	*258*
EVERYONE IN MY NEIGHBORHOOD RECEIVED THE NOTICE	*339*
EVERYTHING WAS ONE ONCE	*573*
EVOLUTIUON, BABY!	572
EXORCISING THE PAST	410
EXPLOITED TO FEEL LOVED	24
EZRA'S ACROSTIC	411
FAINTING STEPS	288
FALLING APART	306
FALLING ASLEEP ON MY SOFA ON A SATURDAY AFTERNOON	196
FALLING IS RARELY IF EVER COMPLICATED	*475*
FAMILY KISSES	123
FAMILY REUNION	412
FASHION FOR ME A GARDEN FROM THIS ROAD	*496*
FAST AS STILL	*247*
FATHER TIME	414
FEAR	415
FEAST OR FAMINE	416
FIFTEEN EPIGRAMS FOR NO ONE IN PARTICULAR	417
FINANCIAL PLANNING	*140*
FINDING SOMEONE WHOSE	*214*

FIRESIDE WINE	443
FIRST AND LAST	117
FISHING WITH DAD	115
FIST	420
FLAG, YOU ARE NOT FLUNG	*209*
FLAME, FLICKERING IN MY EYE	*163*
FLUX	421
FOOLS' FRIENDS	26
FOR ANY RECOLLECTION OF A WRONG	*89*
FOREVER YOUNG	257
FOUR, NOT FIVE	422
FRAGILE IS THE THREAD OF LIFE	*509*
FREE FALLING	423
FREE YOUR MIND	239
FRIENDS ABOUND GATHER 'ROUND	*218*
FROM A BOAT UPON THE GREEN AND ROLLING FIELDS OF THE SEA	*425*
FROM A BOAT UPON THE GREEN	425
FROM DIAPERS TO DIAPERS WE MAKE OUR WAY	*383*
FROM THE TOP	426
FRUSTRATION	338
FUMBLING WITH CHANGE: FOOTPRINTS ON THE WALL	220
G.A.S. (GRANDMOTHERS AGAINST SPEEDERS)	143
GIFTS FOR A MURDERER	427
GIFTS YOU CAN'T BUY	27
GIVE ME A VACUUM FOR MY BRAIN	*177*
GIVING UP	428
GOD'S LAST INSULT TO HIS OWN CREATION	*206*
GOLDFISH	147
GRANDPA'S HANDS WERE OLD AND TWISTED	*361*
GRANDPA'S HANDS	361
HAIKU SUNSET	429
HAIKU! GOD BLESS YOU.	*148*
HALF YES, HALF NO, HALF STAY, HALF GO	297

HALF?	25
HANDSOME MAN	*167*
HAPPINESS	430
HAPPY BIRTHDAY, ROOM 202	29
HARD HABITS TO BREAK	307
HARVEST OF SHAME	81
HARVESTED FROM THE SOIL AS A WEED	*81*
HAS ANYONE SEEN MY LOVE	*25*
HATEMONGERS	280
HE CHALKS HIS PROBLEMS ON THE BOARD	*523*
HE DREAMED OF RISING IN A NEW YORK FLAT	40
HE DRIVES THE NEWEST CARS	*242*
HE HAD THE BRAWN	*190*
HE IS AN OGRE OF THE MOONLESS NIGHT	*235*
HE IS WELLBORN AND WELL BRED	*135*
HE SANG WITH ABANDON IN HIS VOICE	*521*
HE SITS WITH THE BEST YEARS FOR PROCREATION BEHIND HIM	428
HE STUMBLES IN	*288*
HE WHO ADMITS WHEN HE IS WRONG IS WISE	431
HEADS OR TAILS?	195
HELPLESS	354
HER ALABASTER BREASTS	*321*
HERE AT THE BOTTOM IT DOESN'T GET ANY LOWER..	501
HIGGLEDY-PIGGLEDY	432
HIS OLD SOUL HEAVY WITH SEVEN YEARS COMPRESSED INTO	*446*
HISTORY DOESN'T DICTATE DESTINY.	*255*
HISTORY	255
HOITY-TOITY	135
HOLLOW WORDS OF NO INTENT	*254*
HOLLOW WORDS	254
HOLY MACKEREL	98
HOOKER	321
HOW A BOY BECAME A POET	433

595

HOW AN OBSTACLE'S PERCEIVED	*155*
HOW IS A BUILDING BUILT, SON?	*563*
HOW PETTY I FEEL AT THE SEA	*48*
HOW SWEET THE CRUST STOLEN FROM THE COOLING PIE	*46*
HOW SWEET THE CRUST	46
HUMAN SHEEP	*164*
HUMMING AT THE FREQUENCY OF THE HUMAN HEART	*76*
HUNGER AND DEFEAT	258
I ALONE	2
I AM NOT THE POET NAMING	*435*
I AM NOT THE POET	435
I AVERT MY EYES AND PURPOSELY DEPRIVE MY SENSES OUT OF	*552*
I BELIEVE A DAY IS NOTHING MORE THAN A SERIES OF DECISIONS...	*436*
I BELIEVE	436
I BELONG TO A FAMILY IN WHICH THE WOMEN	*123*
I CAME ACROSS A SNAIL	*207*
I CONCILIATE MY FEELINGS	*326*
I DIE	30
I DON'T KNOW IF YOU'LL LIKE THIS POEM	*39*
I DON'T WATCH GERALDO	*127*
I DOUBT	31
I DREAMT THAT I RETURNED TO YOUTH	*108*
I ENVY	32
I FLY	100
I FORGET	33
I FOUND MYSELF IN THE EYES OF A WRINKLED STRANGER	*178*
I GAVE NOTHING WHEN I COULD	*240*
I GIVE YOU THE LIGHT OF MY LIFE	*259*
I GRIEVE	34
I GROW MORE LIKE MYSELF	*185*
I HAD OTHER PLANS FOR MY LIFE	9
I HAD OTHER PLANS FOR MY LIFE, YOU KNOW	*9*
I HATE COLORS	326

Title	Page
I HAVE A LOUSY ATTITUDE	385
I HAVE CONCLUDED	507
I HAVE FOUND THAT CHAMPAGNE	153
I HAVE HEARD STORIES ABOUT CORPSES	316
I HAVE LEARNED	35
I HAVE WALKED BEYOND THE CITY LIGHTS	35
I HOPE	36
I IMAGINE IN THIS CONCRETE WORLD	54
I IMAGINE	54
I KNOW THAT ONE	322
I LEARN MORE ON SUNDAY MORNINGS THAN I DO ALL WEEK	166
I LEARN MORE ON SUNDAY MORNINGS	166
I LEARN	38
I LIKE SHORT POEMS BEST	570
I LIKE THIS POEM	39
I LIKE THIS STANZA ALREADY	539
I LIVE TO SLEEP	134
I LOATHE THE EGOTISTICAL	408
I MADE YOUR PERFUME FROM PETALS	282
I MET A FOUR ONE MORE THAN THREE	440
I MIGHT	41
I REALIZED THAT THE BEST WAY TO ENLARGE YOUR PENIS	130
I REMEMBER ONCE WHEN DAD AND I WENT FISHING	115
I REMEMBER STORIES	488
I REMEMBER WHAT YOU SAID	168
I SEE SOMETHING MOVING OUT OF THE CORNER OF MY EYE	232
I SEE THE SEA NO MORE	325
I SOLD THE WORLD	544
I SPEED HOME	386
I STOP SWEATING	56
I STRAIN	111
I THIRST	43
I WALKED AMIDST A PLANE OF PESTILENCE	318

I WANT TO BE ADDUCTED BY ALIENS 439
I WANT TO PITCH CAMP ON YOUR EGO 426
I WILL PILLAGE 305
I WILL PROBABLY NEVER TELL YOU 263
I WONDER IF EVER I'LL CHANGE MY WAYS 362
I WOULD SAY HE WAS AROUND SEVENTY 57
I, PRONOUN 45
I.R.S. AUDIT 439
I'LL BE RIGHT BACK 438
I'LL USE GOOD FOR WELL 253
I'VE LISTENED TO A RUSTED HINGE 568
I'VE READ AND RE-READ EVERY WORD. 23
I'VE TAKEN TOO BIG A SIP OF COFFEE 403
ICE-DIVIDED PANES 313
IF I COULD THROW A FOOTBALL WITH PRECISION 458
IF I FIDDLE WHILE ROME BURNS 63
IF I LIVE TO SEE TOMORROW 571
IF I LIVE TO SEE TOMORROW 571
IF I NEVER LOVE AGAIN 443
IF I TRAVEL ON THE WINGS OF THE MORNING 562
IF I WERE BLACK 42
IF I WERE BLACK 42
IF ONLY EARTH HAD A SPIN CYCLE 249
IF TODAY IS A GIFT 311
IF YOU'RE GREEDY IT'S TRUE 140
IF YOU'RE LIKE A LOT OF AMERICANS 368
I'M COAXED TO SLEEP 219
I'M IT 277
IMPOSTER AT THE END OF ALE 519
IN A PLACE WHERE STERILITY TEETERS 11
IN AN AGE WHERE T-SHIRTS ARE BILLBOARDS 6
IN COTTON-CANDY AIR 14
IN LINE AT THE GROCERY STORE 56

IN MY BEDROOM BENEATH THE KITCHEN	314
IN PRAISE OF NATURAL DISASTERS	171
IN PRAISE OF NUMBER ONE	440
IN SPITE OF PLASTIC FLOWERS	262
IN THE CONFINES OF A SHALLOW MIND	184
IN THE PAPER THERE IS A PICTURE OF A MISSING GIRL.	461
IN THE SILENT LIBRARY	351
IN THE SOLACE OF SLEEPLESS MOONSCAPES	251
IN THIS AGE OF DISTINCTION, WHERE.	111
IN THIS DREAM THE AUTHOR OF THE BOOK I COULDN'T FINISH	514
IN VINO VERITAS	55
INDEED, MR. YEATS, MAN HAS CREATED DEATH.	549
INERTIA	442
IN-LAWS	193
INNOCENCE ENDS WITH LANGUAGE; THE ABILITY TO TELL A	451
INNOCENCE LOST	47
INSTANT KARMA	232
INSULT TO INJURY	269
INTENTION WITHOUT EFFORT	82
INTERLUDE FOR RELIGION	323
INTREPID YOUNGSTER	257
IRONY FINDS ME IN THE LIBRARY	351
IS IT HUMAN NATURE TO LOOK BACK	483
IT ALL STARTS WITH THE NEED TO EAT.	407
IT CAME TO ME AT LAST	498
IT DOESN'T GET ANY COLDER THAN ICE	389
IT DOESN'T MEAN THEY WON'T WHEN THEY CAN'T OR THEY	363
IT IS HOW THE FISH CANNOT UNDERSTAND	4
IT IS THE EVE OF THANKSGIVING	366
IT RETRACTS LIKE MEMORY AGED	62
IT SEEMED SO UNTHINKABLE	293
IT WAS THE KIND OF CABINET YOU JUST HAD TO OPEN	129
IT'S ALL ABOUT THE LINE-	576

JANUARY 1, 2001	58
JE NE SAIS QUOI NI QUAND	444
JERK BLUES	358
JESUS DRANK BEER	157
JOB SECURITY	57
JUST A THOUGHT...	284
JUST DO IT	133
KALEIDOSCOPE, SPIN YOUR COLORS	*336*
KANSAS LOVES COMPANY	303
KILL ME NOT WITH SLANTED WORD	*319*
KINDNESS	445
LACKING GENUINE VIRTUE, THE UNTHINKING MAN	*564*
LARVA'S NOT A PRETTY THING	*430*
LAST CHRISTMAS	291
LAST RIDE	446
LATE DECEMBER DAYDREAM	447
LATE FALL AND THE FLY IS FAT.	*365*
LAUGHING AT YOURSELF	*201*
LAWYERVILLE	448
LESSONS	450
LET ME SHOE YOU AND CLOTHE YOU.	*427*
LET THE COMPASS POINT RIGHTLY	*228*
LIES	451
LIKE A BOXER WHO'S TAKEN TOO MANY BLOWS	*503*
LIKE ASKING A WOMAN WHEN SHE'S DUE	*85*
LIKE FORTUNES LOST THROUGH POCKET-HOLES	*442*
LIKE STEPPING OFF A SIDEWALK AND GETTING CLIPPED BY A CAR	*102*
LIKE THE FATE OF A TWO-LEGGED TABLE	*388*
LISTEN, ALL MY CHILDREN, THESE ARE THE DAYS OF OUR LIVES	*560*
LITTLE BOY, WITH KNAPSACK TIED	179
LITTLE PINK COAT	11
LIVE, LIVE, LIVE, LIVE	229
LIVING IN THE PAST	452

Title	Page
LONELINESS IS THE DEEPEST SUFFERING I HAVE EVER KNOWN	298
LONGING FOR RECESS	121
LONGING	453
LOST SHEPHERDS	454
LOVE AND WINE HEIGHTEN TRUTH BY NUMBING INHIBITION	139
LOVE AND WINE	139
LOVE IS . . .	214
LOVE LETTER FROM A LAWYER	455
LOVE'S CORNERSTONE	169
LUNACY OFTEN OBSCURES MEANINGFUL INSIGHT.	411
MADNESS, THAT EXPLOSION OF DORMANCY	367
MAGGOTS	60
MAGIC SEEMED MY FATHER'S SPECIALTY	405
MAGNUM OPUS	59
MARCIA'S FACE WAS OILY	95
MARRIAGE IS AS NATURAL AS A CAGED BIRD	457
MARRIAGE	457
MATHEMATIC SOUNDS	264
MAY SOMETHING ALWAYS GO UNSOLVED	36
MAYBE I COULD MAKE A MILLION	458
MEET AND THE PEOPLE SPEAK AND THE PEOPLE LAUGH AND THE	376
MEMORIES OF THE GAME	119
MEMORY'S COMPLEXION	178
MENSTRUAL PERIOD	138
MERRIMENT IN THE DOSE	459
METAPHORICALLY SPEAKING: A BASEBALL PLAYER MEETS A	122
MIDNIGHT STROLLS ON BACK-COUNTRY ROADS AND CARS	215
MILTON DOESN'T MIND THE DARKNESS AT THE BOTTOM OF THE	574
MISSING	461
MISTAKE REALIZED AT EIGHTEEN	462
MOM, CAN I	152
MONDAY MOURNING	360
MOST ARE INCLINED BY HABIT	164

MUCH TIME PASSED.	*8*
MY CAPISTRANO	97
MY CLOTHES FLY FIRED SKIES	*325*
MY DAUGHTER'S CRY IS ON THE EDGE OF SHRILL	*491*
MY DAYS AND NIGHTS REVOLVING	*170*
MY DEAR, HEREINAFTER YOU, MAY THIS LETTER SERVE AS FULL	*455*
MY DOG DOES NOT BLUSH	231
MY DOG WANTS TO WALK	*550*
MY EDEN'S AURA	186
MY FOE OUTSTRETCHED BENEATH THE TREE	*548*
MY FRIENDS	218
MY HEART, MY HEAT, MY WONDER	62
MY HINDU FRIEND TELLS ME THAT	*398*
MY HUSBAND WAKES EARLY	*203*
MY LIFE, IT SEEMS, A BOOK OF DAYS	*226*
MY MAMA WAS A FUNKY DIVA	*309*
MY MIND	*268*
MY MOTHER TELLS ME WITH BOURBON BREATH THAT	*99*
MY NAME HAS DIE IN IT.	*30*
MY NEUTERED DOG	137
MY OWN RELIGION	463
MY PARAKEET HAS THE SNIFFLES.	*391*
MY PARTICLES WILL COALESCE	28
MY PURSE STRINGS STUNG.	*26*
MY SEVENTH GRADE ENGLISH TEACHER TAUGHT ME THAT	*487*
MY SISTER USED TO CRACK NUTS WITH HER TEETH	*222*
MY SOLDIER BOY, SO FRESH FROM SCHOOL	*310*
MY SWEET STILL LOVES ME	113
MY WOEBEGONE FRIEND	*291*
NAMES	464
NERO'S ANACOLUTHON	63
NEVER MIND	148
NEVER TEST THE DEPTH OF WATER WITH BOTH FEET	465

NO CIRCLE SO SOUND	267
NO LONGER WHEN YOU TOUCH MY LEG	*93*
NO MATTER HOW CLEVER OUR MACHINES	*175*
NOAH	467
NONE OF THIS IS TRUE	*61*
NOT A SINGLE SQUIRREL SINGS IN PRAISE	*494*
NOTHING MADE CAN LAST, NOTHING WROUGHT CAN STAY	470
NOUN: THE TEMPERAMENT	*138*
NOW AS AGO	471
NOW NEITHER SPADE NOR PLOW WILL SPLIT THE GROUND	*522*
NURSE!	102
NUTCRACKER	222
O CHARLIE BOY	276
O SACHET, LET OUT GRANDMA'S SMELL	*328*
OBSTACLES & PERCEPTION	155
ODYSSEY OF THE ANT	472
OF ALL THE LESSONS	*450*
OF ALL THE POEMS I HAVE WRITTEN, THIS IS PERHAPS THE	474
OF ALL THE SENSES ONE COULD LOSE	*394*
OF CALAMITY I HAVE SUNG	*165*
OF COMPLICATIONS FROM A FALL	475
OF LEADERS PAST AND PRESENT I'VE LEARNED	*261*
OFF ONE ODD OAK OAR	566
OH, THE BOOKS I OWN BUT HAVEN'T READ	476
OH, YOU RAGTAG RIFFRAFF HOI POLLOI	*390*
ON OCCASION OUR FATHER WOULD SEND HIM	454
ON THE HORIZON	225
ON WHAT'S ABOUT TO HAPPEN NEXT	477
ONANISTIC INTERLUDE	578
ONCE THE CLOUDS WERE UNATTAINABLE	*332*
ONCE WAS WHEN	*1*
ONE ACROSS: SEE SIX DOWN...	*149*
ONE RACE: HUMAN	336

ORDER AMID DISORDER OR DISORDER AMID ORDER?	478
ORDER	478
OUR CHILD, THIS ISTHMUS BETWEEN US	462
OUR LOVE, OUR LOVE	183
OUR UNWANTED GUESTS HAVE GONE.	193
OUT OF A MOTHER'S WOMB	191
OUT OF LIFE ITSELF	65
PACKED MY THINGS TODAY	334
PACKING THE POETS	574
PACKS	337
PARADISE	64
PASS SOON AWAY	265
PEACHY	479
PEARLS BEFORE SWINE	480
PENCILS, PENS, PAPER	481
PEOPLE ASK ME	495
PERFECT CHOICE	206
PERHAPS I THROW THE STONE INTO THE LAKE	270
PERSPECTIVE	483
PHYSICAL	70
PI	484
PICK A NUMBER, A OR B: MATH IS NOT MY FORTE	484
PLOUGHSHARES	69
PLUCK IT FROM THE GROUND.	262
PLUS SIGN	198
POEM IN POEM	380
POET'S BLOCK	485
POISONED SEEDS: THE WAIF, THE WHORE, THE SOCIETY	315
POLITICIANS QUIBBLE	161
POLITICS AND RELIGION	252
PORK CHOPS	486
POSTCARDS FROM HELL	216
PREPOSITIONS ARE WORDS YOU SHOULDN'T END SENTENCES	487

PRIDE, YOU PEBBLE IN MY SHOE	*533*
PRINCESSES AND PEAS	202
PROMONTORY	287
PROUD AS ONE	209
PUT A CORK IN IT	66
QUEST EONS	197
QUIBBLING TIMES	161
QUOD ERAT DEMONSTRANDUM	261
RACCOON	488
RAIL-SPLITTER	489
RAPETURE	330
RATHER TO HER DISMAY	*87*
READING THE DEAD POETS	490
REALLY NOW, WHAT IS A CEMETERY	*546*
REARVIEW NAP	491
REASON FOR REPENTANCE	266
RECOVERING	324
REGRETS	278
RELICS	67
REMEMBER THE PAST	*402*
REMEMBERING CHILDHOOD	270
REST YOU WELL	*250*
REVERSAL REHEARSAL	245
RICHARD CORY'S BROTHER	492
RIGHT DOESN'T COME WITHOUT DUTY	*260*
RIGHTS	260
ROTTEN MILK	333
RUBBLE TROUBLE	200
RUSH-HOUR DREAMS	493
SADNESS IS THE POET'S INK	*77*
SAVE THAT BEAST CALLED MAN	494
SAYDOBE	244
SAYING YOU ARE INTELLIGENT BECAUSE YOU HAVE A DEGREE	*244*

SCHOOL OF HARD KNOCKS	495
SEAM-SIDE-IN OR SEAM-SIDE-OUT	*530*
SEA-WINE SESTINA	496
SECONDS EVOLVE INTO MINUTES	*278*
SEPARATION	314
SERENDIPITY	498
SHADOWS AND AFRICAN AMERICANS	320
SHARING YOUR BLINDNESS	250
SHE ASKS ME WHERE I'VE BEEN	*306*
SHE FEELS HIS DANK THRUSTS	*330*
SHE HAS ONLY ONE LUNG	*337*
SHE LAY DOWN	*236*
SHE LAY WITHERED	*29*
SHE LOVED NOT ME BUT MY MONEY	499
SHE SAID GOOD-BYE	311
SHE SAYS I'M LAZY	*486*
SHE'S THIRTY-NINE	*223*
SHOULD ANGELS BE	*216*
SHOULD I STAND BEYOND EARTH'S LAMENTATION	*84*
SHOUT	500
SHRINKING BACKYARD	356
SILENCE BROKEN	*18*
SILVER LINING	501
SIMILE	71
SINCE I WISH	*156*
SITTIN' ON A PARK BENCH	*358*
SIX A.M. AND THE TRAIN	*317*
SKIN-DEEP	*557*
SKINNY	142
SLANT	319
SLEEPWALKING AT CHRISTMASTIME	116
SLICE OF LIFE	182
SMUGGLERS' DENIAL	92

Title	Page
SNOWGLOBE	502
SO HERE IT IS, THE LONG-AWAITED	58
SO LIKE CHILDREN ARE THE AGED	243
SO SOFT AND LOW THE SWALLOWS GO	97
SO THIS STRAY DOG IS YOUR NEW FRIEND	24
SOME SAY THE WORLD'S FROM THE BIBLE	192
SOMEWHERE BETWEEN HELLO AND GOOD-BYE	297
SPACE	582
SPACE IS QUITE PERPLEXING	582
SPLIT DECISION	503
SQUIRREL INDECISION	53
STARING THROUGH INOPERABLE WINDOWS TINTED A SLIGHT	422
STARVING THE CROWS	339
STEALING EMILY	504
STEPPING IN YOUR OWN GUM	85
STICKS AND CLOTHES	150
STILLBIRTH	203
STONE WISDOM	507
STONES WE'VE THROWN	508
STRAPPED	279
STROLL THROUGH SUMMER'S GREEN	380
STUNTED BY YOUR APATHY	304
SUCCESS OR FAILURE? THAT DEPENDS.	195
SUICIDE: A PERMANENT SOLUTION TO A TEMPORARY	352
SUICIDE?	146
SUPPOSE YOU TOOK A WALK	379
SURELY THERE IS SOMETHING MORE WORTHWHILE THAN HOPE?	37
SWEET SACHET	328
SYLLABLE COUNTER	350
T.G.I.F.	509
TANGERINE	578
TEACH THE CHILDREN WELL	331
TEARS SMEAR BLACK AND WHITE	322

TEATIME DAYDREAM	510
TEENAGE LOVE	93
TELL ME, LITTLE WOODCHUCK SNIFFING THE WIND	*248*
TEST	511
THANK YOU FOR CARRYING MY BURDEN FOR SO LONG.	*445*
THANK YOU	176
THAT HE LIKES MY SHOES	*5*
THAT'S TOUGH.	*114*
THE ADULTERER WAKES AND ASKS THE NIGHT	*73*
THE ADULTERER WAKES	73
THE ANGLES OF THE WINTER SUN	*559*
THE ANIMALS SPEAK OF MAN	513
THE ANSWER TO YOUR QUESTION	74
THE ANT ON THE OPENED ATLAS ON MY ROLL-TOP DESK	*472*
THE ANTS HAVE FOUND A CURIOUS SAND FROM WHICH TO BUILD.	*542*
THE AUDACITY OF THE PETULANT	*575*
THE AUTHOR'S VISIT	514
THE BABY SITS.	*333*
THE BARDS OF YESTERYEAR REPOSE IN MUTENESS.	*490*
THE BARN	517
THE BE-ALL, END-ALL.	*83*
THE BEAUTIFUL, MERCILESS LADY	519
THE BEGINNING	1
THE BLADE OF BIAS	230
THE BOOMERS' BABIES PAID FOR TOMORROW'S HIT PARADE	*561*
THE CAMERA WINKS ITS CYCLOPTIC EYE AT ME	*537*
THE CARDINAL AND THE WORM	521
THE CENTURIES CLOSE, ONE AFTER ANOTHER	72
THE CHASM	299
THE CIRCLE OF LIFE	165
THE CLOSING	335
THE CLOTHES GO ON AND THE CLOTHES COME OFF.	*112*
THE COFFEE'S COLD IN LAWYERVILLE—THE SOUP, TOO	*448*

THE COLORS GO 'ROUND	*249*
THE CORD	522
THE CROWD THINS	*353*
THE DAY DRAGS BY	*196*
THE DECK SHIMMERED, A SEA OF MACKERELS	*98*
THE DEEPEST SUFFERING	298
THE DIMINISHED PUPIL	*523*
THE DIRT OF THE DAY COLLECTS BENEATH MY NAILS	*20*
THE DUST OF A MILLENNIUM	*41*
THE EBB AND FLOW, THE WAX AND WANE, THE FLUX OF.	*421*
THE EGG DRIBBLES ITS	*429*
THE EYES OF MY CHILD	*147*
THE FACE OF A CHILD	*395*
THE FACES OF CHILDREN ARE SO FAMILIAR	*50*
THE FINAL TOLL: A FAREWELL TO LIBERTY	283
THE FLASH FLOOD HAD TURNED CRACKS INTO DITCHES	*299*
THE GAMBLER'S LAMENT	*524*
THE GORILLA LUMBERS TO THE WINDOW	*104*
THE GORILLAS' SIDE	*104*
THE GRAPES OF FUTURE HANGOVERS HANG IN THE CALIFORNIA	*66*
THE GRASS HAS TAUGHT ME	*417*
THE GRASS UPON THE BATTLEFIELD	*525*
THE GUY IN THE MOVIE IS ABOUT TO MAKE A BIG MISTAKE	*477*
THE HANDS GO ROUND	246
THE HEART OF THE MATTER	75
THE HUNGER OF HOPE	37
THE HUNGRY WAVES	*48*
THE IDLE MINDS THAT LUSTED	*283*
THE INCOMPLETE WORKS, PLEASE	*526*
THE INDISTINGUISHABLE	*447*
THE LAST BUBBLE WARBLES TO THE SURFACE	*538*
THE LAST COWBOY	295
THE LAST TIME MY FATHER LEFT	110

THE LAST LAUGH	584
THE LAZARUS EFFECT	564
THE LIFE, AN ACHE, AN ITCH	160
THE MACHINE	76
THE MAGIC CONFLUENCE	106
THE MAGIC KITE	108
THE MAGIC WORD	527
THE MARROW OF MIRTH	201
THE MEASURE OF SUCCESS	281
THE MEMORY OF HIS MOTHER'S FACE	*100*
THE MEN IN THE MIRROR	78
THE MIDDAY SUN	*38*
THE MONUMENTS WE ERECT TO OURSELVES	*470*
THE MORNING GROUND-FOG, THICK AND SOUPY	*517*
THE MOTHERS' TREASURED BABES	*280*
THE MOURNING AFTER	357
THE NAKED BIRCHES STAND	*34*
THE NEWS DEPRESSES	*189*
THE NIGHT HE PACKED HIS SUITCASE HIS SHOES WEIGHED	*110*
THE ONE THAT GOT AWAY	79
THE ONLY TIME I OPEN MY MOUTH IS TO SWITCH FEET.	*252*
THE ONLY WAY I'LL GET TO HEAVEN	528
THE OPRAH WINFREY SONG	127
THE PARADOX OF SOCKS	530
THE PERSUASION OF SANCTIMONY	212
THE POEM ITSELF, HOWEVER, WILL NOT BE LONG	*474*
THE POET'S INK	77
THE PROTRACTED SILENCE OF OUR ARGUMENT HAS LASTED NOW	*378*
THE PUBLISHER WANTS	529
THE QUESTION EVERYBODY ASKS IS WHY?	*384*
THE QUIET MUSIC OF MADNESS	531
THE REASON MEN REPENT IS CLEAR	*266*
THE RELICS OF YESTERDAY'S WISDOM LIE IN SHARDS	*67*

THE REPERCUSSIONS OF GLUTTONY AND INDOLENCE	*91*
THE REST	83
THE RIGHT WAY TO HOLD A FORK	*532*
THE RULES	253
THE SAND WILL OUTLAST MY INTENTIONS.	*174*
THE SCULPTOR'S SCULPTURE'S A ROCK.	*133*
THE SEA SWELLS.	*400*
THE SEASON'S A-TURNING	*80*
THE SHAPE OF LOVE	213
THE SIX RESTRAINTS	533
THE SNAIL'S ANSWER	207
THE SPACES BETWEEN	10
THE SPOUT NOT COOLED SPLATTERS	*277*
THE SQUIRREL IS ALWAYS CROSSING THE ROAD.	*53*
THE SUN ALSO RISES, BUT WHY?	181
THE SUN DOESN'T RISE	225
THE SUN WAS . . .	*33*
THE SWASHBUCKLERS ARE RARELY IF EVER HAPPY.	*10*
THE TERM DEFIES SENSIBILITY	*396*
THE THIRD CANDIDATE	535
THE THRUSHES' THREE	80
THE TIGHTROPE OF REGRET	536
THE TIME ON SOMEONE ELSE'S WATCH	289
THE TOILET SEAT	136
THE TOWN AN ETERNITY AWAY: A BOY ON A FARM	273
THE TRUTH ABOUT THE PAST	537
THE TWO OF US ARE SPLIT	*399*
THE VERY END	538
THE WAIF I NEEDN'T KNOW	*315*
THE WAR IN KOSOVO	*176*
THE WATER DOESN'T KNOW	183
THE WHEREWITHAL OF A MOTHER	*59*
THE WHOLE WORLD STOPPED WHEN I JUMPED FROM REASON	*256*

THE WINNER AND THE WHINER	162
THE WISDOM OF THE BUMPER STICKER	397
THE WORLD IS...	21
THERE ARE MANY KINDS OF ARMS AND LEGS	581
THERE ARE TWENTY-TWO OF US IN THIS ROOM.	511
THERE IS A CERTAIN SOLITUDE	265
THERE IS A POEM I SHOULD HAVE WRITTEN	485
THERE IS AN ECSTASY	202
THERE IS IN LIFE TOO LITTLE TIME	444
THERE IS TRUTH IN WINE	55
THERE'S A FLOWER IN A MEADOW	64
THEY ARRESTED HIM IN THE PARK	531
THEY HAVE EATEN THE BREAD OF AFFLICTION	60
THEY KEEP IT SO PERFECT, THE LITTLE PEOPLE LIVING	502
THEY LIVE IN A HOUSE	370
THEY MUST HAVE THOUGHT HIM CRAZY, THE OLD CODGER	467
THEY SAY HE IS FIXED	137
THEY SAY IF YOU HIT	360
THEY SAY THE AVERAGE MAN	134
THIS A BIG DAY IN HEAVEN	327
THINKING IS HARD WORK	154
THIS IS GOOD	510
THIS IS LIKE TALKING TO MY WIFE	539
THIS IS MAINE IN THE UNPREDICTABLE WINTERTIME.	94
THIS PROMONTORY HAS IT OVER ME	287
THIS TWELVE-YEAR-OLD IS LOST	356
THIS, THAT, THESE AND THOSE	45
THOUGH TREES BE MIGHTY, TALL, AND STRONG	555
THOUGHT UPON SEEING A BAREFOOT BOY	316
THREE MORTAL VERSIONS	191
THRENODY ON LOSS	84
THRESHOLD	268
THUNDERBIRD DREAMS	156

Title	Page
THUNDER'S SONNET	235
TIME IS CONSTANT.	584
TIRED OF THE CEREMONIAL?	463
TO BECOME UN-ANIMAL	106
TO CLOSE MY EYES FOR DEATH	43
TO COME CLOSE, TO BE RIGHT THERE, WITH THE END IN SIGHT...	577
TO HOME	493
TO NEW ENGLAND FROM ENGLAND WE CAME RELUCTANTLY	540
TO NEW ENGLAND FROM ENGLAND	540
TO QUELL THE SANGUINE HEART	269
TO REFER TO NATURE AS ANYTHING BUT OURSELVES	409
TO TAP INTO MY MIND	529
TODAY'S ALREADY YESTERDAY	547
TODAY'S POETRY	576
TOE-TO-TOE BECAUSE WE CAN'T SEE EYE-TO-EYE	392
TON UPON TON UPON TON	293
TOO GAY GROW THE FLOWERS	96
TOO MANY PEOPLE LIVE IN THE PAST	410
TOO MUCH SAKI	541
TRACKS	86
TREASURES WITHOUT KEYS	82
TROUBLES ARE PASSING	352
TRUST	563
TWENTY-FIRST-CENTURY ANTS	542
TWO LITTLE THINGS	175
TWO FIGHTERS	162
TWO INHALATIONS	141
TWO O'CLOCK: TIME FOR A SHAKE AND A DRIBBLE	286
TWO SONS	290
UNDERSTANDING	241
UPON READING AN AD FOR PENIS NLARGEMENT	130
UPON RETURNING TO ELEMENTARY SCHOOL	543
UPON RETURNING	543

USED GOODS	544
VALET PARKING, TIE REQUIRED	*545*
VEGETABLE LOGIC	131
VENI, VIDI, VEGGIE	545
VERSE SCIOLTI DA RIMA	546
VERTIGO FROM THE LADDER'S TOP RUNG	*572*
VILLANELLE FOR LAURIE (MY SISTER FOUND A GRAY)	87
VINEGAR AND WINE	210
VITA BREVIS	547
VOICES TRAPPED IN SILENCE	*500*
VOYAGE	355
W.B.	548
WAITING	549
WAKE ME FOR DINNER	118
WALKING ON WATER	89
WALKING THE DOG	550
WAR'S OTTAVA RIMA	551
WE ALL FALL DEAD	68
WE ARE GOOD AT FINDING LITTLE TRUTHS	*65*
WE GIVE VALUE TO THE PEARL	*480*
WE HAD DEVISED PLAYS EVEN THE NFL HADN'T SEEN	*119*
WE LIVE, AS GENERATIONS HAVE AND WILL	*284*
WE OFTEN REFUSE THE TRUTH	*92*
WE SANG "RING AROUND THE ROSY"	*68*
WE SHOULD HAVE BEEN A-GIVING	240
WE SNEAKED OUT OF YOUR BEDROOM	*220*
WE TWO LONELY FOOLS	552
WE USED TO HAVE THE BEST DISCUSSIONS, MY FATHER AND I	*17*
WE WOULD GET ALONG	*241*
WEEP FOR ME NO MORE	553
WEEP FOR ME NO MORE, THOUGH SORROW'S SO DEAR	*553*
WHAT AM I BUT A SYLLABLE-COUNTER	*350*
WHAT DOES HUMAN SAY?	554

WHAT I CAN'T TELL YOU ABOUT MY FAMILY IS THE STUFF YOU	377
WHAT IF I COULD PAINT A PICTURE WITH WORDS SO KEEN	19
WHAT MEMORIES OF SLOW-ROLLING PLAINS	273
WHAT SUBTERFUGE IS THIS, O HEART	329
WHAT THE EARTH IS WORTH	555
WHAT'S NOT REAL	16
WHEN HE DIED	357
WHEN I AM DEAD	556
WHEN I AM DEAD, MY SWEETHEART	556
WHEN I FOUND THE PLAYBOY	129
WHEN I WAS Y1K	275
WHEN ONE BEER LEADS TO TWO	157
WHEN QUESTIONING WHY I HAD TO MAKE MY BED	375
WHEN RICHARD CORY'S BROTHER WENT DOWN TOWN	492
WHEN SHE'S ONLY BEAUTIFUL	557
WHEN SOME EXCAVATOR FINDS MY BONES	12
WHEN THE CHOSEN TWO-FACEDLY FORSAKE	294
WHEN THE MAGIC OF CHRISTMAS IS A HALF-OFF SALE	27
WHEN THE PAST KILLS THE FUTURE	90
WHEN THE TRUTH COMES OUT	153
WHEN TO REST WE LAY THE WORLD'S SWAY	558
WHEN UNTO HEAVEN MY SOUL IS TAKEN	194
WHERE HAVE YOU BEEN?!	151
WHILE MY ELDER NEIGHBOR FILLED HIS PANTRY	416
WHILE THE PARTY DANCED ON WITHOUT ME	583
WHO AM I AMONG SOME SIX BILLION NAMES?	464
WHO CAN TELL US HOW WE SHOULD LIVE?	15
WHO LEFT THESE TRACKS IN THIS FRESH SNOW?	86
WHY DO WE DO THIS, THIS PERIODIC GET-TOGETHER	412
WHY DOES HE TORTURE HIMSELF	513
WHY I DON'T DO CROSSWORD PUZZLES	149
WHY I GOT IN TROUBLE AS A CHILD	152
WHY IS IT THAT I'M ALWAYS GETTING STUCK BEHIND THAT	143

WHY PEOPLE COMMIT CRIMES	150
WHY WOULD THERE BE A SECOND THOUGHT?	*438*
WILL SOMEONE GET RICH FROM MY WORKS WHEN I'M DEAD	*526*
WINTER'S CHARITY DEAD	*279*
WITH SNOW-LADEN LASHES AND RUBY-RED LOBES	*113*
WOODCHUCK	*248*
WORDS LABEL UNTIL THEY OFFEND	44
WORDS OF INSPIRATION FROM A SOAP OPERA STAR	560
WORKING IN MY GARDEN TODAY	*271*
X SPEAKS	561
X	190
Y2K	275
YEARS AGO	*290*
YES, I SAID OF THE LIGHT BEAMING FROM MY EYES	528
YET ANOTHER WINTER IS UPON ME	453
YON YEN	91
YOU CANNOT HOLD YOUR BREATH	245
YOU HAVE DONE THIS BEFORE	*536*
YOU LOOK JUST LIKE YOUR FATHER	17
YOU PERSISTENT, PESTERING MOSQUITO	338
YOU SAID THE TRAIN HAD JUMPED ITS TRACKS BECAUSE IT WAS	489
YOU SHOULD RIGHT YOUR WRONG.	239
YOU SPEAK OF DOGMA	233
YOU STARED AT ME, YOUR MIND DRIFTING AWAY	404
YOU STOOD LIKE A FOG	90
YOU TRIED TO BE A FREE MAN TOO SOON	210
YOU WONDER WHAT THE HELL IT'S ALL ABOUT	74
YOU, ROBERT FROST	567
YOU'RE CLIMBING WITH FRIENDS IN ARIZONA	423
YOUR FACE I'VE NEVER SEEN	289
ZEBRAS IN THE ATTIC	332
ZERO IN ON THE ONE AND ONLY	580
ZERO TO YOU IN TEN SECONDS	580

www.ingramcontent.com/pod-product-compliance
Lightning Source LLC
Chambersburg PA
CBHW030236170426
43202CB00007B/24